Brave Histories & Hopeful Futures:
Voices of a Refugee Community
Volume 3

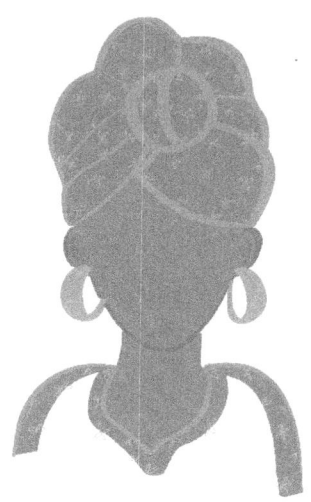

Written by:
Students at Refugee Hope Partners

Raleigh, North Carolina

Brave Histories & Hopeful Futures: Voices of a Refugee Community

A Collection of Writings by Students at Refugee Hope Partners

Copyright © 2024
Literacy & Community Initiative / Refugee Hope Partners
Individual Authors

All rights reserved. This book or any portion thereof may not be reproduced or used in any manner whatsoever without the express written permission of the publisher except for the use of brief quotations in a book review or scholarly journal.

Editor & Literacy & Community Initiative Site Coordinator:
María Heysha Carrillo Carrasquillo

Refugee Hope Partners Founder and Executive Director:
Michele Suffridge

Director, Literacy & Community Initiative: Crystal Chen Lee
Co-Director, Literacy & Community Initiative: Jose Picart

Literacy and Community Initiative
College of Education &
Friday Institute for Educational Innovation
North Carolina State University
2310 Stinson Drive
Raleigh, NC 27605

PARTNERS

DEDICATION

This book is dedicated to the community who loves and supports the student writers.
Thank you for the continuous encouragement.

TABLE OF CONTENTS

Acknowledgments
11   Dr. Crystal Chen Lee
13   Michele Suffridge
15   Angela Lombardi
16   Dean Paola Sztajn
17   Dr. Krista Glazewski
18   Dr. Kevin Oliver

Introductions
19   Dr. Angela Wiseman
20   Anna Christian Allen
21   Maria Geary
22   María Heysha Carrillo Carrasquillo

Chapter 1: Identity

27	I was born on October 3rd	Annointing
29	I was born on March 22nd	Fartun
31	I was born on May 29, 2008	Hapy
33	I was born on January 25th	Idah
35	Moi	Kevine
37	I was born on March 16th	Nyota
39	I was born on May 8th, 2008	Ornella
41	Rebecca	Rebecca
42	About Me	Sarah
43	I was born on July 3rd	Shukum
45	Get to Know Me	Sophia
47	About Me	Wile
49	I was born on November 22nd, 2008	Zawadi

50	I was born on February 23rd	Zoe

Chapter 2: Transparent Journaling
53	Eupiphanie
54	Fartun
55	Hapy
56	Iqra
57	Kevine
58	Ornella
59	Rebecca
60	Salwa
61	Sarah
62	Solange
63	Sophia
64	Wile
65	Zawadi
66	Zoe

Chapter 3: Cultural Vignettes
69	Ramadan	Fartun
70	My Family Reunion	Eupiphanie
71	My Big Booty Judy Long Gone	Annointing
72	Christmas in my Hometown	Hapy
73	Shiny Black Shoes	Idah
74	Eid Day	Iqra
75	Playing in the Rain	Salwa
76	Going to the State Fair	Sarah
77	My Everyday Life	Solange
78	Going to the State Fair	Sophia
79	The Photo Party	Wile

80	Church Life	Zoe

Chapter 4: Opaque Journaling
83	Iqra
84	Kevine
85	Rebecca
86	Salwah
87	Sarah
88	Solange
89	Sophia
90	Wile

Chapter 5: Community
93	LCI Community: Learning and Helping Together	Iqra
94	Teamwork, Teachers, and Ties: My School Community	Kevine
96	The Joy of Learning and Friendship in School	Rebecca
98	Our Family: A Mix of Feelings	Salwa
100	Building Bonds: The Power of Teachers and Friends in School	Sarah
101	Solange's Tanzanian Family	Solange
103	The Transformative Influence of Great Teachers in School Communities	Sophia
104	Life in my Community	Wile

Chapter 6: Affirmation Cards
107	Fartun
108	Iqra

111 Kevine
113 Rebecca
115 Solange
117 Zehra
119 Zoe

Chapter 7: Empathy

124	I am helpful	Fartun
125	In response to Fartun	Kevine
126	Practice makes progress	Iqra
127	In response to Iqra	Fartun & Kevine
128	I am a positive person	Kevine
129	In response to Kevine	Fartun & Iqra
130	I believe in myself	Rebecca
131	In response to Rebecca	Zoe & Zehra
132	I appreciate my opportunities	Solange
133	In response to Solange	Zehra & Zoe
134	I am strong	Zehra
135	In response to Zehra	Solange
136	Singing & I live in joy	Zoe
137	In response to Zoe	Rebecca & Solange

Chapter 8: Vision Boards

141 Eupiphanie
142 Iqra
144 Kevine
145 Ornella
147 Rebecca
148 Salwah
149 Sarah

150	Solange	
151	Sophia	
152	Wile	

Chapter 9: Justice

155	Being a Black Person in USA	Eupiphanie
156	Congo	Eupiphanie
157	School	Eupiphanie
158	People Want Justice	Iqra
159	We Are All Equal	Kevine
160	Injustice has to go	Ornella
161	Justice Should Be Served	Ornella
162	We Are All Equal	Rebecca
163	See Life Clearly Without Our Judgement and Filters	Salwa
164	We Are All Equal	Sarah
165	My Race Does Not Define Who I am	Solange
167	Stop the Violence	Sophia
168	We Are All Equal	Wile

Chapter 10: Activism

171	Dear Faith People	Eve
172	Dear Sanderson	Kevine
173	Dear Students	Rebecca
174	Dear Sanderson	Solange
176	Dear You	Wile

Appendix

178	Author Biographies
193	Project Photos

198   About Refugee Hope Partners
199   The RHP Team
202   About the North Carolina Museum of Art
203   The NCMA Team
205   About the Literacy and Community Initiative
208   The LCI Team
218   About North Carolina State University

ACKNOWLEDGEMENTS

LITERACY AND COMMUNITY INITIATIVE

We are so honored to release this third volume by the talented and brave students of Refugee Hope Partners (RHP). This multimodal book stands as a continued testament to the brilliance of RHP authors and RHP staff members. Their stories, art, and voices are amplified in this book to demonstrate their incredible and powerful journeys as refugee students in North Carolina. This third book demonstrates the ongoing collective stories composed of brave histories and hopeful futures.

In addition, I want to thank RHP and the North Carolina Museum of Art (NCMA) for their partnership and for their human and financial resources in the project. I especially want to thank the RHP Staff for their tireless commitment to students. Thank you to Michele Suffridge, Anna Christian Allen, and Mary Greene for their dedication in pushing this project forward.

I also want to thank Angela Lombardi and Ashlee Moody for their precise organization and commitment to this project through NCMA. Thank you to Maria Geary, our teaching artist, for giving this gift to our community.

I also thank North Carolina State University, the Friday Institute of Educational Innovation, and Wake Promise for its generous funding and its mission to meet the needs of historically underserved populations in North Carolina. Thank you to Jose Picart and Angela Wiseman, two wonderful faculty collaborators.

A special thank you to LCI's research assistants, María Heysha Carrillo, Haven Hall, and Hannah Savariyar for their detailed work in leading, teaching, and editing this project. Another thank you to Demet Seban, for her participation as a visiting scholar. This work would not be possible without them. Their passion is an inspiration to witness.

It is with great honor and immense gratitude that we present this third Refugee Hope Partners publication filled with writing and art— we hope it inspires us all to learn from these students' brave histories and hopeful futures.

Dr. Crystal Chen Lee
Founder & Director, Literacy and Community Initiative
Associate Professor, North Carolina State University

ACKNOWLEDGEMENTS

Refugee Hope Partners (RHP) exists to engage, equip, and encourage refugee families so that all may thrive. RHP serves over 1300 refugees from 49 different countries living in Raleigh, NC. Our programs focus on four holistic pillars of service: education/enrichment, health/wellness, faith/community, and advocacy/equipping.

The impact of RHP's partnership with LCI is clear. Throughout this school year, a group of students from our diverse community worked alongside an inspiring, encouraging, and supportive LCI staff. The LCI framework of write, engage, and lead empowered these students to find, embrace, and develop their unique voice.

Although many students' stories have roots in violence, displacement, and shame, the LCI program provides students with tools to reframe these stories into ones of strength, overcoming, and hope. As students find power in their words, they feel confident to share their written works within the community. The community is changed through these resilient students' courage and leadership. We are thankful for LCI's commitment to the youth of RHP and look forward to a deeper partnership in the future!

Michele Suffridge
Founder and Executive Director, Refugee Hope Partners

ACKNOWLEDGEMENTS

It has been an honor for the North Carolina Museum of Art to partner with LCI and have the opportunity to meet the amazing young women involved with the program at Refugee Hope Partners. It was inspiring to see their creative expressions expand from writing to visual art under the care of artist Maria Geary. They demonstrated their individuality through their creations, and we valued the trust they put into the process. Their visit to the museum was a wonderful experience, enabling more of our staff to meet them and share the collection with them. We hope they will continue to visit us and find the NCMA to be a place of peace and reflection in the years to come.

Angela Lombardi
Director of Outreach and Audience Engagement
North Carolina Museum of Art

ACKNOWLEDGEMENTS

NC STATE UNIVERSITY

The NC State College of Education's land-grant mission is to make a transformative impact on society and advance the greater good. The Literacy and Community Initiative exemplifies that mission through the partnerships it fosters and the outreach it provides to empower youth and amplify their voices. This book, *Brave Histories of Hopeful Futures, Volume 3* reflects LCI's invaluable contributions in giving youth spaces to be heard and seen. We know creating these spaces is important to advancing diversity, equity and inclusion so all learners have the opportunity to thrive. I am inspired by all that the LCI team — led by Associate Professor Crystal Lee, Professor Jose Picart, and Associate Professor Angela Wiseman — has done to create these spaces and lift up our youth's voices. I am also inspired by the brave, smart, and resilient students whose writing you will read in this book. I am proud they will help shape our society's future.

Paola Sztajn
Dean, NC State College of Education

ACKNOWLEDGEMENTS

NC STATE UNIVERSITY Friday Institute for Educational Innovation

The mission of the Friday Institute for Educational Innovation is to advance K-12 education through innovations in teaching, learning and leadership enabled by collaboration among a wide range of stakeholders. The Literacy and Community Initiative (LCI), led by Dr. Crystal Lee, Dr. Jose Picart, and Dr. Angela Wiseman is an exemplary program that embodies this mission. Through their partnerships with community-based organizations, the LCI team and their work helping students find and elevate their voice truly demonstrates an innovation in teaching, learning, and leadership that the Friday Institute is proud to support. We are honored to endorse their latest publication, *Brave Histories and Hopeful Futures: Voices of a Refugee Community Volume III*, by the students at Refugee Hope Partners and are grateful to be even a small part of this truly impactful work. In exploring the personal narratives collected in this edition, we are given the gift of access to many worlds, journeys, and heroes. I thank the authors for letting us come along.

Krista Glazewski, PhD
Executive Director
Friday Institute for Educational Innovation

ACKNOWLEDGEMENTS

NC STATE UNIVERSITY

The Literacy and Community Initiative (LCI) is an excellent example of university extension into the local community. Their work to empower and amplify the voices of area youth through collaborative publications and leadership opportunities around storytelling and advocacy is both inspiring and impactful. The Teacher Education and Learning Sciences (TELS) department is proud to have some of its faculty involved in guiding the work of LCI along with university partners at the Friday Institute and numerous community partners. The research these teams conduct on their writing/reading initiatives helps to inform broader practice and implementation of LCI's theory of change with documented effects on youth literacy, leadership, and social-emotional outcomes.

Kevin Oliver, PhD
Department Head and Professor
Teacher Education and Learning Sciences
North Carolina State University

INTRODUCTION

In the pages of this book, we witness the magic that unfolds when a community joins together in shared creativity and passion in the form of personal narratives, thought-provoking ideas, and creative artistic visions. To the reader, we invite you to turn the pages and witness so much talent from the youth who have written, painted, photographed, collaged, journaled and sketched images and words. The writing and visual images reflect inequalities, call for empathy, and offer reflections of positive change. Meanwhile, as you read this book, you will witness vulnerability, wisdom, empowerment and insight of youth that reflects their brilliant diversity and life experiences. It should give you hope for the future!

This book serves as a powerful declaration which reflects what we are capable of when we collaborate. I am thankful for the wonderful community partners who came together to guide us through various ways of creating writing, photographs, poetry, and other forms of expression! In this way, this book is far more than a collection of words and images; it shows the very best of what happens when creativity and passion come together. I am proud to be a part of the LCI community!

Dr. Angela Wiseman
Associate Professor of Literacy Education
North Carolina State University

INTRODUCTION

What a beautiful display of partnership and community this whole process has been. With the supportive, thoughtful, and intentional planning of the LCI staff, the refugee adolescents of Refugee Hope Partners have engaged every month in both the writing and art processes, culminating in a beautiful, published masterpiece.

Creating works that center around ideas including community, identity, culture, and empathy, these refugee adolescents have exhibited both *bravery* and *hope*. I believe they are better for creating them, and you will be better for reading them!

We are so grateful for this beautiful partnership between LCI and RHP, and are honored to be a part of this third iteration of *Brave Histories and Hopeful Futures*! Many congratulations to its contributors!

Anna Christian Allen
Director of High School & College Academics
Refugee Hope Partners

INTRODUCTION

From the shyness of our first meetings to the boldness and risk taking in our last, it has been a joy to experience artistic growth in these young women. Meeting monthly to learn, share, and create takes a commitment and they met it head on! In these pages, you will find strength, surrender, determination, character and respect. This book is more than a labor of love: it is a manifestation of collective hope.

Maria Geary
Teaching Artist
North Carolina Museum of Art

INTRODUCTION

In your hands, you hold a treasure trove of wisdom and resilience, a spirited artifact crafted with the strength of lived experience and provoked by reflection. This book is a collection of written words and art pieces crafted by vivacious young people who have faced displacement, navigated new cultures, and challenged adversities to forge their own paths and still had the determination of waking up on Saturday mornings to come WRITE with us.

As lead-project coordinator, I had the honor to lead this artistic journey in various sessions, create the curriculum, and ENGAGE in meaningful activities and dialogues about identity, culture, community, empathy, justice, and activism. I learned with them during Ria's sessions on art journaling, experiencing new mediums and warming up of recently discovered ones. We learned that practice makes perf— progress!

These emerging writers and artists LEAD us in this journey to witness their transformative journeys through honest poems, evocative vignettes, essays, advocacy letters, and dozens of artistic creations. With vulnerability and authenticity, they share their struggles, hopes, and epiphanies, offering us an intimate glimpse into their worlds and hearts.

In the chapters, they reveal some complexities of their self-discovery as students, refugees, adolescents. They celebrate the richness of diversity of thought, religion, family structures, linguistic abilities. Lead us to explore the unbreakable bonds that unify them in this writing community, and allow us to witness the power of raising our voices for self-expression, action and change.

Their words testify to the beauty of embracing our uniqueness and valuing our roots. They transport us to the places that have shaped their identities. They remind us that we are not alone on our journey. They lead us to see examples of how strength is found in connection and mutual support. With passion and conviction, they urge us to confront injustices, fight for equality, and forge a more compassionate world.

This book is a testament to the courage to be heard in a world that often silences marginalized voices. Allow yourself to be inspired by these young writers' resilience and wisdom. Embrace authenticity and diversity, and let the stories of these brave authors guide you toward a deeper understanding of yourself and the world around you. May their words resonate with your being, reminding you of the transformative power of self-expression and the strength that the power of writing in community gives us.

María Heysha Carrillo Carrasquillo, M.Ed.
Lead-Project Coordinator, Literacy and Community Initiative
Doctoral Student, Teacher Education and Learning Sciences
North Carolina State University

Chapter 1

Identity

In this chapter, the young writers openly and honestly reveal themselves to the readers. Inspired by the poem "My Honest Poem" by Rudy Francisco, the authors share their identities and life experiences. Through their personal poems, these teenagers reveal their unique personalities, dreams, fears and more. By connecting in such an intimate way, the writers create a safe space for other young women refugees to feel understood and supported.

I was born on October 3rd
Annointing

I was born on October 3rd
I hear that makes me a happy person
I am not perfect
I'm a sucker for Nepal food

I'm still learning to talk
I'm often quiet
I'm often talkative
I like food a lot

I've been told that I am awkward
People say that I am understanding
Secretly, I'm ready to have a house

I have this odd fascination with the people around me
I assume it's because we are crazy
I know it sounds crazy, but I am ready to move out
And to be honest, I think I'm changing

I know this sounds weird,
but sometimes I wonder if Adam and Eve are in heaven
I wonder what it feels like to be kicked out of heaven
I am afraid that I might be absorbed by the world

Hi, my name is Annointing
I enjoy singing, dancing, and eating
But, I don't allow myself to do what I want

I don't know the future outcomes,

but I do know that God is in control
I know God is watching over me
I know the right man will come when the time is right

I was born on March 22nd
Fartun

I was born on March 22nd
I'm still learning not to be nice
to everyone whom I don't know

I'm often sleeping
I'm often learning in school
I like to sleep and eat

I've been told that I don't look African
People say that I am disrespectful
People say that I look beautiful

I love to draw
I assume it's because I am bored
And to be honest, I don't like new people

I know this sounds weird,
but sometimes I wonder
how God grew the kids in the stomach

I wonder why people judge people
without knowing their stories
I am afraid that I will lose the people that I love the most.

Hi, my name is Fartun
I enjoy being around people that I love
But, I don't allow myself to love them too much
I have someone who cares about me
more than the people I know

I have a dream.

My hobbies are to sleep
I don't know why I am afraid of new people,
but I do know that they are weird.
I know that I am loved
I know that I am beautiful in my way.

I was born on May 29, 2008
Hapy

I was born on May 29, 2008
I hear that makes me a stronger woman
I am more than others think I am
I'm a sucker for doing my homework

I'm still learning how to be confident during a group project
I'm often with people I know in school
I'm often bored at home
I like dancing and singing gospel songs a lot.

I've been told that I don't look my age
People say that I'm fun to play with
People say that I am always smiling
Secretly, I'm not

I have this odd fascination with my homework sometimes
I assume it's because I'm always bored
I know it sounds crazy, but it's true
And to be honest, I'm not that lazy.

I know this sounds weird, but sometimes I wonder why I like scrolling through my phone
I wonder why I'm good at everything I like
I am afraid that everyone will get to know me soon.

Hi, my name is Hapy or Hapendeki
I enjoy dancing a lot
But, I don't allow myself to be seen a lot
I have to love myself
I have to be proud of myself

My hobbies are eating, dancing, and singing
I don't know how to laugh with others, but I do know how to be angry
I know I'm good
I know I'm still good.

I was born on January 25th
Idah

I was born on January 25th
I hear that makes me an Aquarius
I am 5 foot 3
I'm a sucker for delicious food

I'm still learning how to be kind with my words
I'm often sleeping for long hours
I'm often laughing when I should be serious
I like being happy a lot

I've been told that I am funny
People say that I am always eating
People say that I should be a model
Secretly, I do too

I have this odd fascination with taking pictures
I assume it's because I like moments to last long
I know it sounds crazy,
but I end up deleting them
because I don't have enough storage
And to be honest, I will keep taking those pictures

I know this sounds weird,
but sometimes I wonder what my purpose is in life

Hi, my name is Idah
I enjoy eating, playing sports, and being outside
But, I don't allow myself to cry as much as I should

Moi
Kevine

I was born on August 18, 2008
I am 5'1
I'm crazy for boys with a good heart

I'm still learning how to do math
I'm often loud
I'm often quiet
I like sneakers

I've been told that I am a good leader
People say that I'm nice and funny
People say that I'm pretty
Secretly, I don't think so

I have this odd fascination with soccer
I assume it's because I play it
I know it sounds crazy, but I love it.
And to be honest, I hate when people get on my nerves

I know this sounds weird,
but sometimes I wonder if my crush likes me back
I wonder if I am cool
I am afraid that I'm ugly

Hi, my name is Kevine
I enjoy making new friends
But, I don't allow myself to talk first
I have a good heart
I have a lot of friends

I know how to cook
I know how to make people's day

I Was Born on March 16th
Nyota

I was born on March 16th
I hear that makes me a Pisces
I'm a sucker for men with beautiful eyes

I'm still learning how to not laugh in serious situations
I'm often independent
I'm often in my bed
I like spending time with the Man upstairs

I've been told that I'm a good listener and a good advisor
People say that I need to go outside more
People say that I have a contagious smile
Secretly, I want to get married

I have this odd fascination with being alone
I assume it's because I am an introvert
I know it sounds crazy, but I hate pictures
And to be honest, I don't know how to swim

I know this sounds weird,
but sometimes I wonder what heaven is like
I wonder if God considers me one of his people
I am afraid that I might be living a life
contrary to my purpose

Hi, my name is Nyota
I enjoy eating
But, I don't allow myself to overeat
I have a Congolese heritage

I have hope that one day I'll finally be
who God wants me to be

My hobbies are writing and reading
I don't know my future,
but I do know Jeremiah 29:11 to be true
I know I am beautiful
I know who I am

I was born on May 8th, 2008
Ornella

I was born on May 8th, 2008
I hear that makes me a Taurus
I am 5'3, weight 159 pounds
I'm a sucker for a tall boy and have a lot of girls beside him

I'm still learning how to leave people
who do not match my energy or talk bad about me
I'm often quiet when bothered and smile with people I like
I'm often feeling like I need to do something
I like to sleep because it makes me forget about myself
and I do it in the end

I've been told that I'm nice
but at the same time,
people attempt to take advantage of my kindness
People say that the way I act makes me look stupid
for my age
People say that I love too quick and that's gonna ruin my life
Secretly deep down, I'm a nice person
more than how people see me

I have this odd fascination with art
because it makes me disappear from the rest of the world
I assume it's because I love drawing
even though I'm not good at it
I know it sounds crazy, but I like to dress up for no reason
And to be honest,
I love to dress differently from other people
Girls my age wear dresses

but I like wearing pants and shorts.

I know this sounds weird,
but sometimes I wonder
what would happen if I was not nice,
how would anyone treat me?
I wonder what my parent thinks of me
and how my friends see me
I'm not afraid of anything
or what someone has to say about me.

Hi, my name is Ornella
I enjoy sleeping, watching TV, eating, and drawing
I don't allow myself to care about what anyone has to say about me
I have an odd obsession for a boy who is my friend
and someone's boyfriend

My hobbies are driving and riding bikes
I know I'm loved, short, and kind-hearted

Rebecca
Rebecca

Hey guys
My name is Rebecca.
I was born on July 15th, 2008
I hear that makes me a little girl
I am not afraid of anything

I'm still learning how to do math and speak English
I'm often feeling dizzy and tired
I like to sleep and eat.

Sometimes I ask for help
People say that I am nice
and some people hate me
People say that I am not a good person
Secretly, we all just want to be good people

I like to watch movies
I play with my little brother
It makes me happy

About Me
Sarah

I was born on January 1st
I'm a sucker for a tall man with a cute smile

I'm still learning how to not laugh in a serious situation
I'm often loud in places where I should be quiet
I like tall men a lot.

I've been told that I believe too much
People say that I am beautiful
People say that I am weird sometimes
Secretly, I get nervous every time someone gets close to me

I know it sounds crazy,
but some things are easier than it seems.

I know this sounds weird,
but sometimes I wonder what people think about me
I wonder if I'm good enough
I'm afraid of losing someone I love one day.

Hi, my name is Sarah
I enjoy listening to my favorite music
I know I'm beautiful
I know who I am

I was born on July 3rd
Shukum

I was born on July 3rd
I am 4 foot 11
I'm a sucker for men who believe in me

I'm still learning to control my tongue when talking
I'm often hungry
I'm often busy learning new things
I like singing and making friends

I've been told that I'm short for my age
People say that I'm a good singer
People say that I have a nice smile
Secretly, I like to get compliments

I have this odd fascination with running
I assume it's because I play soccer

I know this sounds weird,
but sometimes I wonder what people think about me
I wonder if I am good enough
I am afraid that people think I'm weird

Hi, my name is Shukum
I enjoy singing and playing soccer
But, I don't allow myself to believe I'm not good enough

I have a dream
I have a calling
My hobbies are getting to know people
I don't know much, but I do know it is my life
I know God will help me through everything
I know I'm still working on myself.

Get to Know Me
Sophia

Hi, my name is Sophia
I enjoy listening to music
I have a bad memory

I was born on July 9th
I am 5 foot 1
I'm a sucker for crazy tall dreadheads

I'm still learning how to pass my classes
I'm often quiet in places where I should be loud, but
I'm also often loud in places where I should be quiet
I like Faygo a lot.

I've been told that I am weird
People say that I need to go outside more
People say that I am annoying
Secretly, I get nervous every time a teacher gets close to me

I have this odd fascination with dreadheads
I assume it's because I once had a crush on one of them
I know it sounds crazy, but I am in love

I know this sounds weird, but sometimes I wonder what
people think about me
I wonder how it feels to be loved by your parents
I am not afraid of anything

My hobbies are listening to music
I don't know how to draw,
but I do know how to play the violin.
I know a person that cares about me
more than I care about myself.

About Me
Wile

I was born on January 18th
I hear that makes me a good girl
I am a woman, not a girl
I'm a sucker for tall boys

I'm still learning how to draw
I'm often alone
I'm often kind
I like observing

I've been told that I'm pretty
People say that I'm good at painting

I have this odd fascination with basketball
I assume it's because it looks interesting
I know it sounds crazy, but that's the truth
And to be honest, I'm not lying

I know this sounds weird,
but sometimes I wonder why we need a hall pass
I wonder what will happen
if we go to the bathroom without a hall pass
I am afraid that I might not make it

Hi, my name is Wile
I enjoy being at school sometimes
But, I don't allow myself to speak when I'm not in the mood
I have a weird laugh

I have six siblings and there are nine of us in our family.
My hobbies are listening to music and painting
I don't know how to talk to people,
but I do know how to be friendly
I know that I'm nice and cool
I know all my friends are not nice
and my guy friends are not funny sometimes

I was born on November 22ⁿᵈ, 2008
Zawadi

I was born on November 22nd, 2008
I am a student, I am studying in high school
I'm a sucker for drinking water and Coca Cola

I'm still learning how to be known to speak English
I often like my personal things.
I often love my family and myself
I like to play games and music,
I like my family
and I like to read a lot

People say that they like me and others don't like me.
Hi, my name is Zawadi.

I was born on February 23rd
Zoe

I was born on February 23rd
I hear that makes me a Pisces
I am 4 feet
I'm a sucker for singing

I'm still learning how to control the way I look at people
I'm often alone
I'm often on my bed
I like singing and writing

I've been told that I'm a good listener
People say that I don't have pride
Secretly, I don't have it

Hi, my name is Zoe
I enjoy singing, writing, sleeping
But, I don't allow myself to speak back to people,
I mean I do a bit but it has to be in a respectful way

My hobbies are talking about different voices in singing
I don't know if you love me for the way I am,
but I do know that I love myself for the way I am.

Chapter 2

Transparent Journaling

Journaling is primarily a personal journey, yet there are moments when we share our thoughts to connect with others. We are inherently curious and delving into someone else's writing often sparks conversations that might not have otherwise taken place. Using transparent mediums like colored pencils and markers enables our writings to be visually accessible, prompting conversations to flourish.

Eupiphanie

Hello, welcome here
I love writing because
Back in my country that
how we express our feelings
and it better to
write about it than to
talk about it to anyone.

I love my name because of it
meaning and because it
unique and very special
all over the world

I'm Eupiphanie

it's not like I hate Art,
I just found Art a little
bit boring but it does
bring peace to me.

My middle name is Jasmine
when I came to America
I gave myself a middle
name.

Fartun

My name is Fartun

I don't belive on words at all, I hate when people come out of no where and they know my name. I don't Talk about my feeling at all. I talks about with god, god is someone I can talk about. Sometime I be confuse about god, huh How come, when I am sad I am happy I want to eat I want to I am hugry I want to eat I want to I want to sleep I want to eat I want to eat my mom and I am so sleepy where I bruh whcon are we going to eat I want to sleep I I am hugry I want to eat I want to a Food Food Food Food Food I want to sleep Food Food Food Food Food Food Food Food Food Food Food Food Food Food Food od Food where are Food Food Food to w Food I want to eat Food w to Food Food Food Food Food Food hugy Hi Hi Hi Hi Hi Hi Hi Hi Hi Food Hi Hi Hi Hi Hi Hi Hi Hi Hi Hi Hi Hi Hi Hi Hi Hi Hi Hi Hi Hi Hi Hi Hi Hi Hi Hi Hi Hi Hi Hi Hi Hi Hi Hi Hi Hi Hi Hi Hi Hi Hi Hi

Hapy

Iqra

I grow up in Afghanistan-Pakistan where my mom and dad grow up over there but I grow up in Kube. I have 7 siblings with me. Four sisters three brothers. When I was coming to U.S.A I used to learn english from my older sister. When I come here it was very hard to learn english but I learn it and I am still learning english and spelling words is so hard for me. I am at Sanderson high school freshmen year. I like to cook food for my family. I bake frying, boiling it's fun but sometime it's so hard and it's need pacient to have. One time I fry my middle finger like every single time when I cook. I don't like art but I still give a try but it doesn't work. I love to wear hoodies it's so comfortible. I don't have anything easle to write but I am still writing. I just take abut every have anything so bye bye bye you soly or not but I dont wath see you ok bye hope not to see you

Kevine

I like dancing because it makes me feel better even though I feel shy dancing in front of people but still do and I also like playing soccer with my friends and my friends playing for so I and I love hanging out with my friends I don't even though my don't like ... my ... proud and like school but I still go just to ... my ... I love trying new things like food, clothes, dances.

Love

Ornella

My name is Ornella and I love art. Art is my wrold where I can forget about reality and make me feel better when im at my lowest or when i dont feel like sharing my end of the storie. Art is one subject that ive been doing better ever since i was 3 years old. Art is my life my peace, and my everything.

Again my name is Ornella that girl who wants to be an artist and a designer

Rebecca

Sometime Bati

Napende kol Pizza kwasababu nitamu | Sometime I don't like Pizza because
sipenda kingisi watu wasemanga Jana la | because The put too much chess and
ngu vibaya. Ninapenda family yangu | too much oil
na na penda rafiki zangu.

Salwa

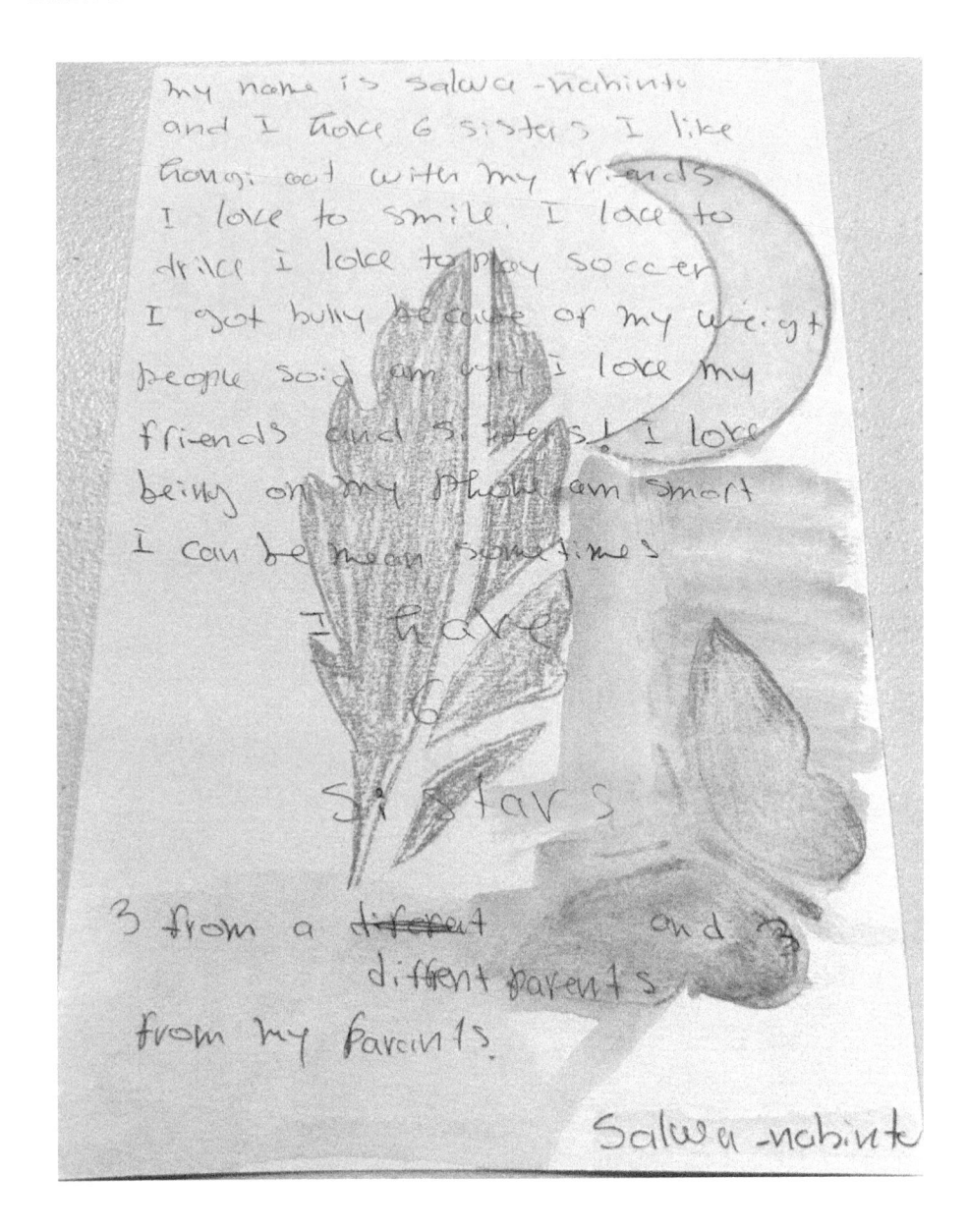

my name is Salwa -nahinto
and I have 6 sisters I like
hangiout with my friends
I love to smile. I love to
dance i love to play soccer
I got bully because of my weight
people said am ugly i love my
friends and sisters! I love
being on my phone am smart
I can be mean sometimes

I have
6
Sisters

3 from a different and 3
diffent parents
from my parents.

Salwa -nahint

Sarah

Solange

During my freshman i started liking this boy i was so delusional about him i needed serious help cause my delusions were to much and like always i take my courage and went to tell him about how i felt and he rejected it was really sad and the depression hit me i became so depressed and overwemed that everything because he was the first guy that we ever actually liked it take me a while to get over the rejection but years later i did and im doing better than ever. and i actually realized that he was not even that good looking it was just me being boy crazy and i basically decided to ignore him like he never existed to me and it was the best thing that ive ever done for myself because i actually cared about myself and realized how much ive always put other people first and not myself and how much i cared about other peoples feelings but never thought about my feelings.

Sophia

I don't like when someone calls me Sofie
I feel good when someone calls me Sophia
why — looking at me what is she saying
me no spanish but what
mind yo own bzness cuse she is crazy
move your hand lady what to draw
la la la la la la la la la la la la la la la la la la la la la la la la la la la la la la la la

Wile

it be funny whenever sister
someone say my name wrong
i mean i say like how this
boy say my name he calls me
William he so funny and cool
i mean some people thinks that
his mean but he not mean to
me i know you guys will be
wondering why you are reading
this but its okay his basically
known as my best person that
i have met this year he so fun
to hang out with i just miss
him so much that i wish he
was here with me i mean
thank god that he live close
so maybe we might see each
other i don't or maybe when
i learn how to drive i will meet
him

Zawadi

- I like to eat rice because I love this food.
- I like school because is my favorite at school is math and Est y science.
- I like to drawing y write y ready.
- my dad my mom and my brothers
- my favorite music is Worship.

Zoe

- my name
- my food
- phone number
- my teacher teller

- my photos gallery
- the way I dress

- the grade I'm in
- my bible name
- my country flag

Chapter 3

Cultures and Countries

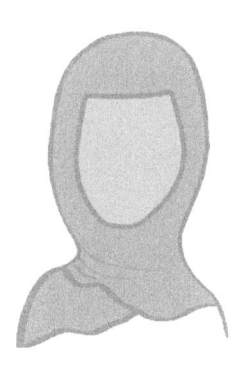

In this chapter, the young writers immerse us in their culture and experiences of living in different countries. They show us how everyday activities can become emblematic of their cultural imaginary. Through their vignettes on culture and country, they demonstrate how culture serves as a vehicle for understanding lived experiences. These vignettes allow us to observe how teenagers who have experienced displacement from their places of origin make meaning and collect memories that sustain them in their lives in the United States.

Ramadan
Fartun

At 5:00, my mom and I start cooking all our cultural food. I smell the onions and spices; they smell amazing. We go get the goods ready. I put the blanket on the floor and my sister will bring the plates and the cups. My dad mixes the avocado drinks. He brings *kochumbari*, a special rice that we make. When we are done pulling out the food, we pray together. It's time to eat! I taste the samosa. It sounds so crispy. I hear my family talking, my sister and brothers laugh, my dad makes fun of my little brother, and we start laughing.

My Family Reunion
Eupiphanie

It was Christmas 2017; my mom and my grandma chose to cook for the whole entire family. When I entered the compound, I smelled the delicious meal that my grandma and my mom were cooking. I saw my family happy and full of joy; when the meal was done, my mom and grandma called for all of us to eat. I tasted *fufu* and *sombe* that my mom cooked. Then, when we finished eating, I went to my mom and dad to say thank you, and I touched my mom's soft hands and my dad's strong hand. Then I heard my mom telling my dad that she loved him, and he said that he loved her, too. It was a lovely gathering for the whole family, and it will always be my favorite memory in my life. I will cherish it all my life and hope this moment can happen again.

My Big Booty Judy Long Gone Annointing

It was a regular day of the week, I was walking back home from a friend's house. As I was walking, I heard running, so I decided to look back, and boom! I found myself running from a dog. I trotted very fast and jumped on the nearest fence. Then I heard an uncanny clamor at the back of my big booty Judy while jumping. I could smell the dog's happiness when it was chasing me, I saw cats, flowers, and houses as if my life was flashing before my eyes. The taste of fear rising from my heart invaded my mouth; the bricks felt like my own life savior, but I managed to escape the horror.

Christmas in My Hometown
Hapy

At first, I was sleeping, and I heard a lot of noise. I went outside, and I saw people saying "Happy Christmas" and laughing together, and I asked what was going on. Is it the same day? Yes, it was still the same day (they shouted at me), saying, "It was Christmas, dummy" (*gasps*). I went back inside, got water, and poured it out. It was the best day ever. Then we went to my grandma's house because we always got ready at her house. We celebrated there for a few hours, and we called all our cousins to come and play some music together. I then went to church and praised the Lord for saving us... because it is a special day for people we know and we come together after church. I tasted a lot of things that we have in common (and people always give little kids money!), and it is always a good time when we get money from our parents. I touched a lot of things like good people's hair. When things were good, I heard people singing, dancing, and eating. People were singing great. I smelled some food like rice, beans, and drinks.

Shiny Black Shoes
Idah

It was like any other day of the week; wake up, get ready, and go to school. That was the routine. However, this day felt more peaceful than watching the sunrise from the shore. I had woken up so early that even the sun was not awake, but I was. After waking up, I trotted my weary body to the bathroom, washed my face, brushed my teeth, and took my morning leak. I felt more energized and ready for the day. Next, I put on the same red sweater, blue dress, red socks, and shiny black shoes. For breakfast, I had the same tea I would drink every morning.

Eid Day
Iqra

On Eid day, we wake up early in the morning. One by one we take a shower, pray, dress up, and go to the *masjid*. We pray the Eid prayer, and we hug each other to celebrate. After that, we get some snacks, and we go home. My uncles and my dad gives us Eidie (money)--however much they want to give us. After we get our Eidie, we eat breakfast and decorate our house.

Greeting together with families on Eid day is special. Twice a year my families get together to celebrate this day. My uncles and my brothers grill the chicken, and my aunties and my mom cook the rice and beef, and provide more food for people to bring home with them. After we eat the food and drank green tea, all my uncles, brothers, cousins, me, and my older sister play cricket together.

At night, we all get together in one house. We pray together, and after we pray, we drink green tea, talk, dance, and sing together.

Playing in the Rain
Salwa

Thirty minutes after I came back from school, it started to rain. My friend and I decided to play in the rain. We were playing in the rain, and we could smell rice and *sombe*. We saw people playing Horo and we went and joined them. We touched the sand. Tt was wet because it was raining. We heard people screaming but it was happy screams. We went to my friends' house, and we took a shower and changed our clothes. We ate *sambusa* and *sombe* rice!

Going to the State Fair
Sarah

When the State Fair was in North Carolina, I wanted to go there. My friends and I were going to go together but we couldn't. So, I had to go with people I didn't want to go with.

When I got there, I saw people playing games and eating. I smelled hot dogs, meat, and chicken wings. I touched a chair and a table. I heard people talking and music. I tasted mango juice and pizza. It wasn't fun because I went late at night and none of my friends went with me.

My Everyday Life
Solange

Every Monday morning in Africa at 8:00, I get ready to go to school. I went to school from Monday to Saturday. On Saturday, it was cleaning day. We girls cleaned the bathroom and the classrooms, and the boys only picked up trash on the floor. On Sunday, I wake up and get ready for church. I hated it cause the walk was too long and tiring and that's exactly what I did every day.

Going to the State Fair
Sophia

Going to the State Fair with my siblings was an adventure. In the beginning, it was hard because the parking lots were all taken. The only ones that were left were the ones to pay for, so she had to pay because she didn't have any choice. Then we went in and rode the rides. I smelled food there, but most was seafood. I saw a bunch of people. I tasted crabs, and they were salty. I touched the toys around, and I heard people screaming. We only had one ticket each, so we had to pick a ride we liked. I picked the ride. I told my sisters about the ride, and they agreed, but then we had to go in. While we were on, I heard my little sister crying. I couldn't do anything other than laugh. Then she suddenly stopped crying. Good thing she was next to me because I opened my eyes to find out that she passed out and that was the funniest part that I found myself crying. Two minutes later, the ride stopped and then she woke up. We were all dizzy even the driver AKA my sister. We ran out of tickets, so we had to go back home.

The Photo Party
Wile

I was so happy to hear that we had homecoming, but at the same time, I was worried that my mom would not let me go. It took me a minute to think if she would say no or yes. I waited till she got in a good mood, and finally, I had the courage to go and ask her. She agreed because it was at school, and I was happy. I went and got ready for the photo. When I was done getting ready, we pulled up to the party, and it was so much fun. I didn't even want to go home, but really, I had to go home. But again, the party was fun.

Church Life
Zoe

The drums were already playing when we walked into the church. I have my Bible in my hands. I take a seat and they call my group to stand up and sing. We go to the stage, I take a microphone and my brother holds the guitar, we start to sing songs. We start with *Tupate Kwarani*. After that, we sing *Niralo Swali,* and after singing, we go back to our seats. The pastor starts to preach after we sing again and then it stops right here. Everyone is going home; some are going to eat and going to visit their friends.

Chapter 4

Opaque Journaling

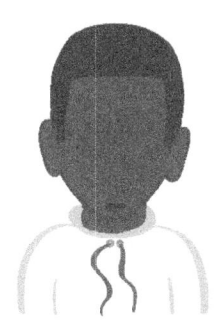

Each person carries stories within them that may not be ideal to tell. With acrylic paint, these narratives can be veiled, concealing any hurt, shame, or disappointment they hold. These stories don't require verbalization; rather, they can be buried beneath layers of stenciling, patterns, and artistic designs, keeping them safely concealed. By "releasing from within" through our writing, we not only process these experiences but also create art that fosters a more positive impact atop these buried stories.

Iqra

Kevine

Rebecca

Salwah

Sarah

Solange

Sophia

Wile

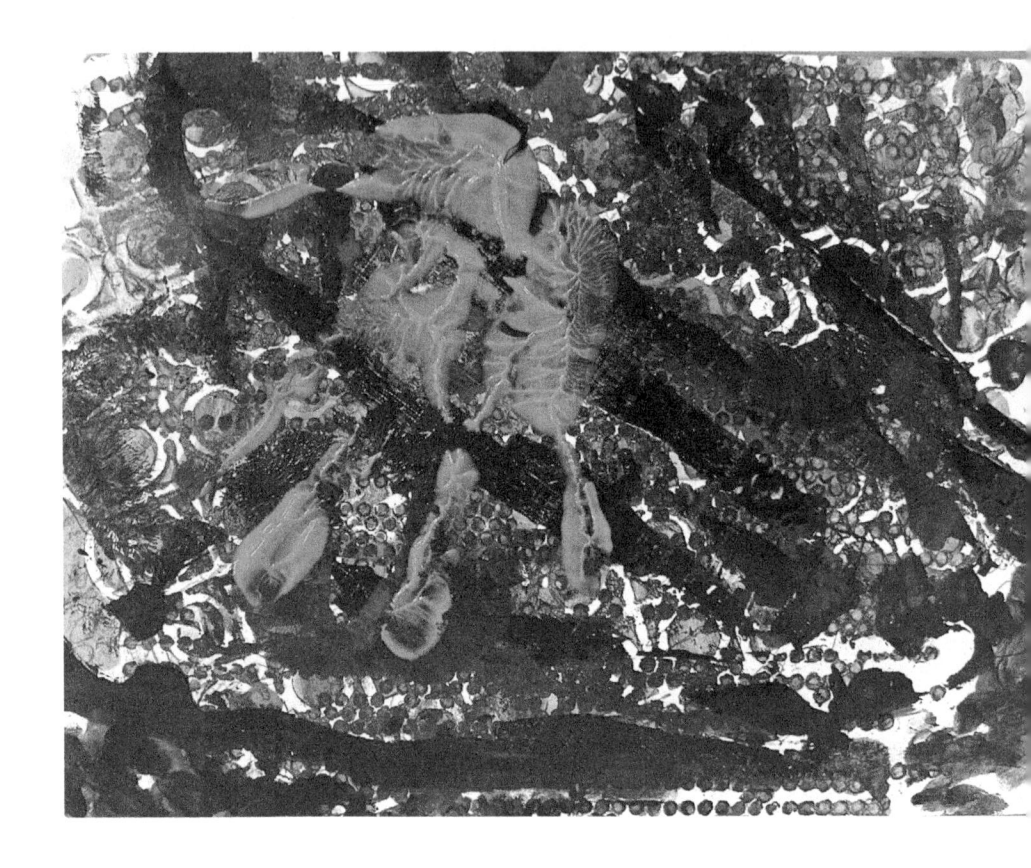

Chapter 5

Community

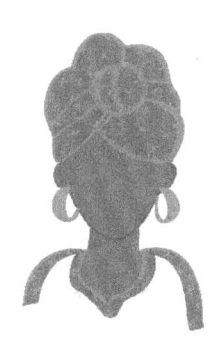

In this chapter, the young writers use the essay genre to explore the theme of community. Through various examples of communities in their lives, the authors describe the functioning of these communities - whether school, family, or created out of affinity as teenage refugees in the United States. They analyze the practices that unite and strengthen these groups, highlighting what they most appreciate about belonging to them. They also reflect on the transformative power of community life and the benefits it brings to their lives. As part of this writing process, the writers experimented with and used Chat GPT to help them draft essays using their ideas and notes.

LCI Community: Learning and Helping Together
Iqra

Our LCI community is like a big family where we all learn, help each other, and get inspired. When someone has a tough time, we step up and say, "We help each other when we struggle." This makes us strong because we face challenges as a team, turning problems into victories that we celebrate together.

In our community, we love learning and writing. Each person adds something special to our shared knowledge, making it grow. "Teach us new things" is like our motto. It means we're always ready to learn from one another. Here, everyone can be a teacher and a student, and that makes our place full of exciting discoveries.

Our community is like a story that we all write together. Every message, every idea, is like a stroke on our canvas of shared experiences. "Teach us new things" isn't just a saying; it's an invitation to explore and be curious. It's what makes our community a cool place where everyone helps each other learn and grow.

In the big picture of our LCI community, we're more than just individuals. Together, we're a strong team. We stand united, always learning, collaborating, and inspiring one another. Our community is like a friendly guide on our journey of learning and growing, reminding us that when we come together, we can achieve amazing things.

Teamwork, Teachers, and Ties: My School Community
Kevine

School is more than just classes; it's a place where I've learned, made friends, and discovered a diverse world. My school community has been a great journey, marked by teamwork, exciting learning, a helpful teacher, new friendships, and exposure to different languages.

I love working with my classmates. We share ideas, help each other, and learn together. It's not just about books; it's about understanding different perspectives and becoming a team.

School isn't just about memorizing facts; it's about exploring and thinking. From interesting discussions to fun experiments, my school makes learning exciting and helps me grow.

I'm lucky to have a teacher who makes tough things easy to understand. This teacher isn't just someone who gives lessons; they're like a guide, helping me feel confident and passionate about what I'm learning.

My school is a place with lots of different people. Meeting friends from various backgrounds teaches me about the world. We learn to appreciate each other's differences, making our school a welcoming place for everyone.

In my school, I get to hear and learn new languages. It's not just about words; it's about understanding different cultures. This experience helps me see the world in a bigger way.

My school community is a special place. It's where I work with friends, learn exciting things, get support from a great teacher, make new friends, and explore different languages and cultures. This journey is not just about grades; it's about becoming ready for the exciting and diverse world outside of school.

The Joy of Learning and Friendship in School
Rebecca

In the bustling cafeteria of our school, a heartwarming scene unfolds daily as students gather to share lunch, laughter, and learning. This daily ritual is a testament to the vibrant community that thrives within the walls of our school.

The lunch period is more than just a time to nourish our bodies; it is a celebration of friendship. Students from diverse backgrounds come together, creating a mosaic of personalities and stories. As we sit around tables, plates filled with food, conversations flow. It's a time to catch up on the latest happenings, share anecdotes, and simply enjoy each other's company. The joy of being with friends is evident in the smiles and camaraderie that fill the air.

Amidst the friendly chatter, learning doesn't take a backseat. The collaborative spirit extends beyond the lunch tables into the classroom. Students engage in discussions, listening attentively to teachers and peers alike. The exchange of ideas and knowledge becomes a dynamic process, making the classroom a place for intellectual curiosity.

Texts and writing assignments are embraced with enthusiasm. The rustling of pages and the tapping of keys create a symphony of academic engagement. Students eagerly dive into the world of literature, dissecting texts, and expressing their thoughts through writing. This shared academic pursuit not only fosters a love for learning but also strengthens the bonds between classmates.

The love for our friends and the joy of learning are not confined to the classroom alone. Running, laughing, and playing together create memories beyond textbooks and exams. School becomes a place where friendships are nurtured not only through shared academics but also through the simple joys of play.

In conclusion, our school is more than just an educational institution; it is a community where the joy of learning and the warmth of friendship intertwine. From lunchtime gatherings to classroom discussions and playful moments on the school grounds, every aspect of our school experience is a testament to the bonds we forge and the knowledge we share. In this environment, we not only grow academically but also personally, cherishing the friendships that make our school days truly special.

Our Family: A Mix of Feelings
Salwa

In our family, we feel lots of different things. Sometimes, we're happy and supportive; other times, we face tough moments. Our family story mixes coolness, niceness, meanness, annoyance, happiness, amazement, loudness, fighting, love, and stress. Our house is very full, and we have a big family. I live with my mom, my aunt, and my uncle. I have 3 sisters and 23 cousins.

Our family has good times when we support and celebrate with each other. But, like all families, we also have tough times with arguments and hurtful moments. We need to be strong and talk about our feelings to make things better.

We annoy each other sometimes, like when we tease or have funny habits. But, in the end, happiness comes from shared laughter and good times, showing how much we care about each other.

Our family is full of different talents and interests, making things exciting. We're also a loud bunch, cheering for each other and having lively discussions. It's like having a lot of energy and passion in our home. This happened when we are watching a movie together and we start laughing about nothing

We argue sometimes, but it's a part of being close. Through conflicts, we learn and grow, reminding us of the strong love that keeps us connected. Sometimes we just fight about things like when I get a bad report from school or when I don't do things right when I come home late.

Life can be stressful, with lots of problems. But, as a family, we face challenges together, supporting each other and making things easier.

Our family story is special because it's a mix of feelings and experiences. We learn, laugh, and face tough times together, creating a story that's uniquely ours. Even if we aren't together later, I will always remember them.

Building Bonds: The Power of Teachers and Friends in School
Sarah

In a wonderful school, teachers are like superheroes. They not only teach us lessons from books but also teach us about life. They care about us and make learning exciting.

Having good friends in school is like having a second family. They make the school days fun and help us through the tough times. We laugh, study, and share everything together.

School can sometimes be stressful, but a great school helps us deal with it. They teach us how to handle stress, offer support when we need it, and create a peaceful atmosphere where we feel safe.

When teachers are like friends, friends are like family, and stress is manageable, school feels like a second home where we grow, learn, and become better versions of ourselves. It's these things that make our school community so special and close-knit.

Solange's Tanzanian Family
Solange

In the heart of Solange lies a Tanzanian family that embodies the true essence of togetherness. As the sun sets over the horizon, casting warm hues across the savannah, this Tanzanian African family gathers in their humble abode to share laughter, love, and the simple joys of life.

One of their cherished rituals is the shared laughter that goes through the room while watching TV. The television, a window to the world beyond, becomes a focal point for the family to unwind and enjoy moments of light-hearted entertainment. The genuine, hearty laughter creates an atmosphere of warmth, binding the family members in shared happiness. It is during these moments that the bonds between them are strengthened, and the stresses of the day are momentarily forgotten.

Equally significant are the celebration occasions, where the family comes together to prepare food for special events. The kitchen, a place of spices and shared stories, becomes a hub of activity. Each family member contributes to the preparations, seamlessly blending tradition with the joyous anticipation of the festivities ahead. As they chop vegetables, stir pots, and share family recipes, the air is filled with the good scents of the cuisine and the sounds of laughter and conversation.

Communication in this Tanzanian family is not just about words; it's about the rhythm of shared experiences. As they work together in the kitchen, a silent understanding develops—a glance, a smile, or a shared nod conveying more than words ever could. The elders pass down age-old culinary secrets, while the younger members bring in a fresh perspective, creating a harmonious fusion of generations.

Celebrations, whether big or small, are not just about the destination but the journey undertaken together. The laughter, the shared tasks, and the unspoken communication during these moments forge memories that linger long after the celebrations have ended.

In the heart of Tanzania, this family reminds us of the universal language of joy that transcends cultural boundaries. Through the simple acts of watching TV and preparing food together, they demonstrate the beauty of shared laughter and communication, weaving a tapestry of love that defines the true essence of family life.

The Transformative Influence of Great Teachers in School Communities
Sophia

Great teachers inspire students with their passion for learning and subject matter. Beyond academics, they serve as mentors, providing guidance and instilling values that contribute to students' holistic growth.

Great teachers embrace innovative teaching methods to cater to diverse learning styles. Their adaptability cultivates a spirit of continuous improvement, preparing students for the dynamic challenges of the modern world.

In celebrating great teachers, we acknowledge their transformative role in shaping both the academic achievements and character of students, fostering a positive and inclusive school community.

Life in My Community
Wile

Our church is more than a place to pray; it's where we connect every Sunday and support each other. We're all about being together and enjoying life. We love to dance – for special occasions or just for fun. It's our way of celebrating and showing that we're all friends here.

When it comes to food, we treat cooking like an art. The kitchen is where we share family recipes and make meals with lots of love. Potluck dinners and community feasts are times when we all enjoy good food together.

Laughter is what keeps us close. We love to laugh together, telling jokes or just being silly. Making each other laugh is our way of spreading love and staying connected.

Chapter 6

Affirmation Cards

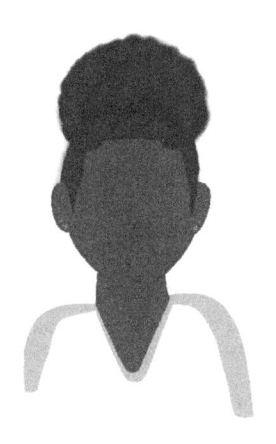

We need positive affirmations to help us achieve goals, build confidence, and change the negative sound bite that sometimes rewinds and repeats. It's how we learn to speak things as though they are and not perceived to be. Positive affirmations are our simple truths!

Fartun

I am helpful
I live in worries
I give up easily.
I love myself

Iqra

Today is a perfect day

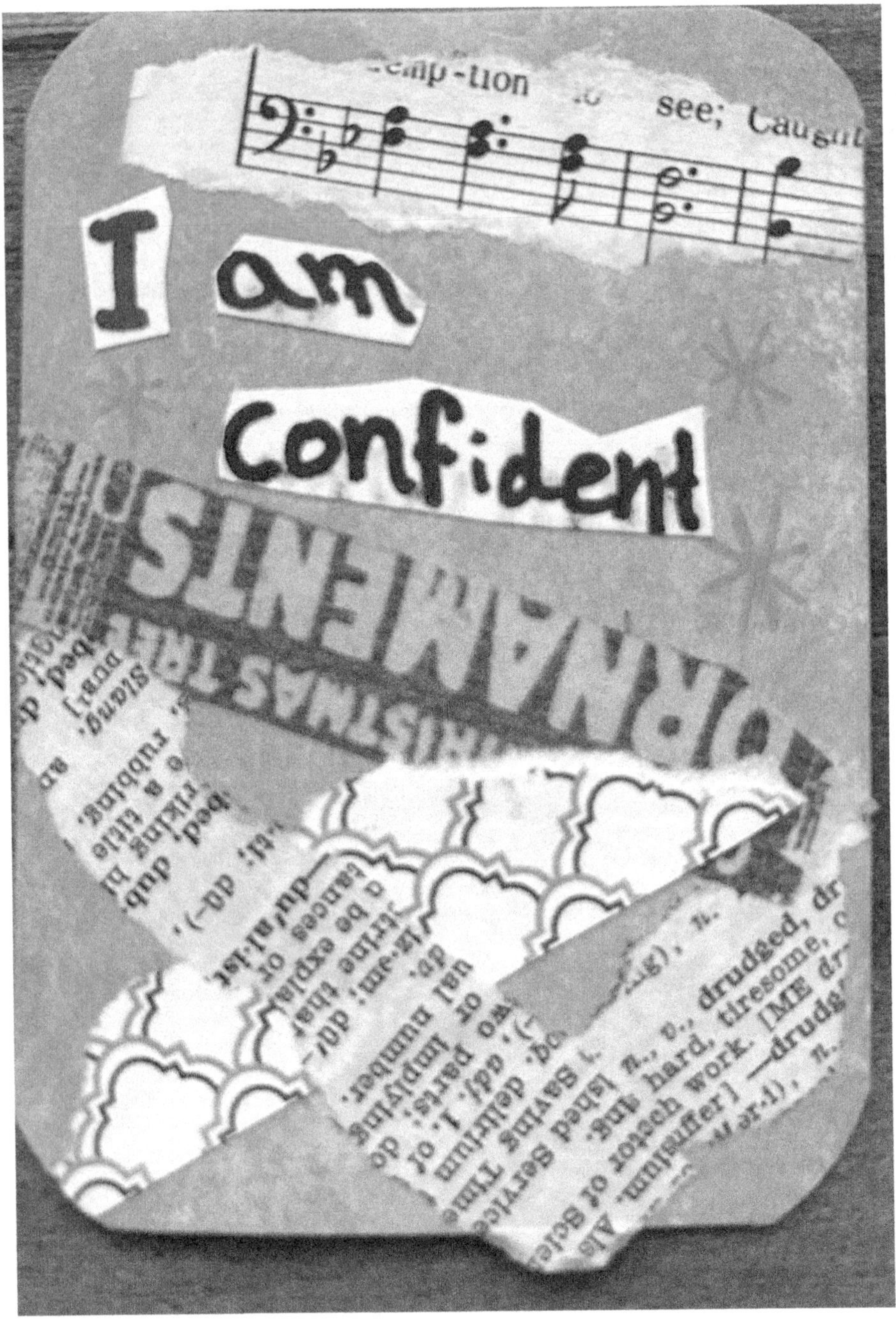
I am
Confident

Kevine

> I am AMAZING!
>
> My opinion matters
>
> Practice makes progress

- I am strong
- I appreciate my opportunities
- I am a positive person
- My body is healthy
- I can reach my dreams
- I believe in myself

Rebecca

I can reach my dreams

I believe in myself

these sim - ple men;
as Je - sus called;
to him with joy
in var - ied ways

Solange

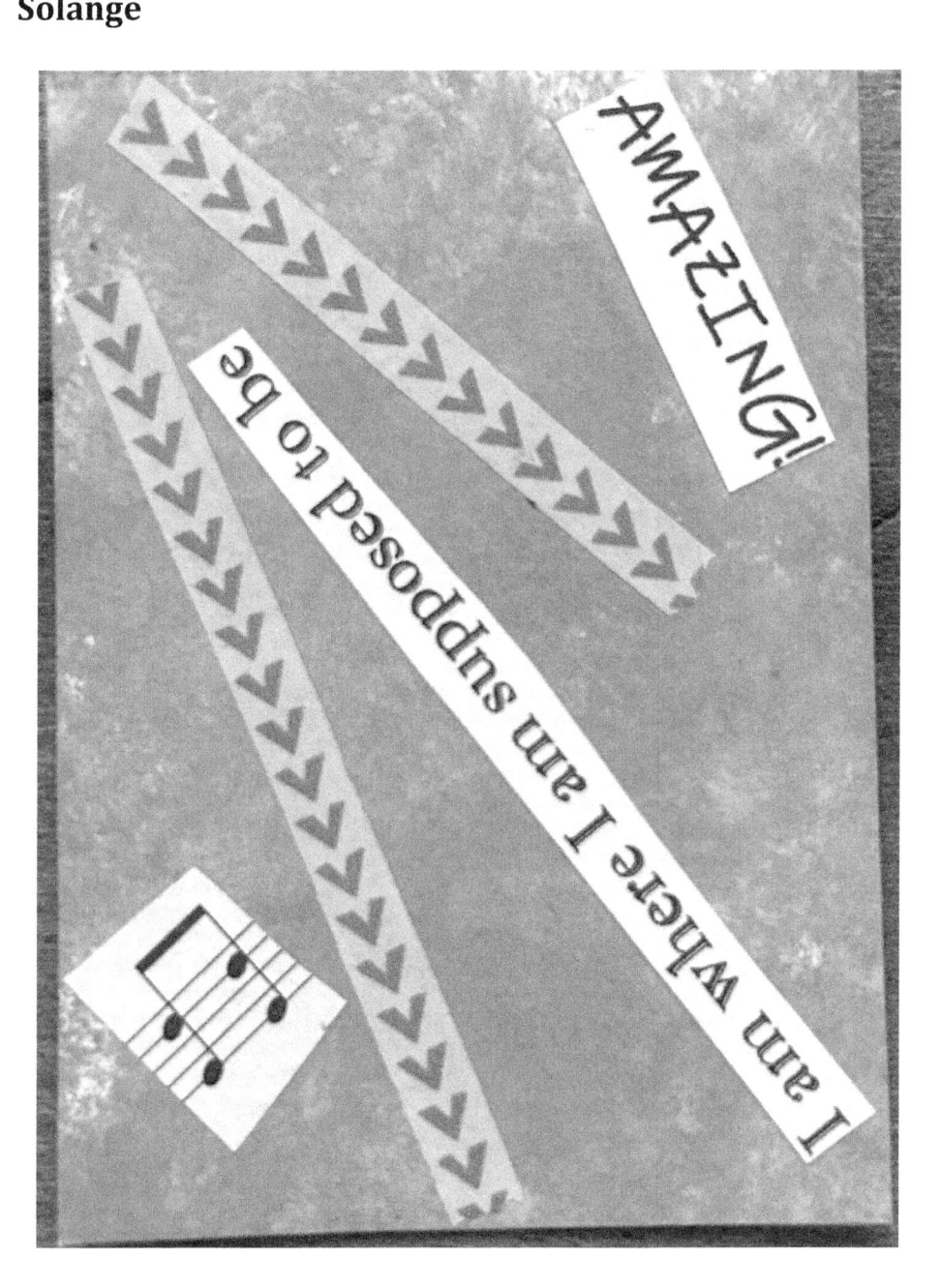

I appreciate my opportunities

I live in joy

I am beautiful inside and out

My soul is fulfilled

I am worthy

Zehra

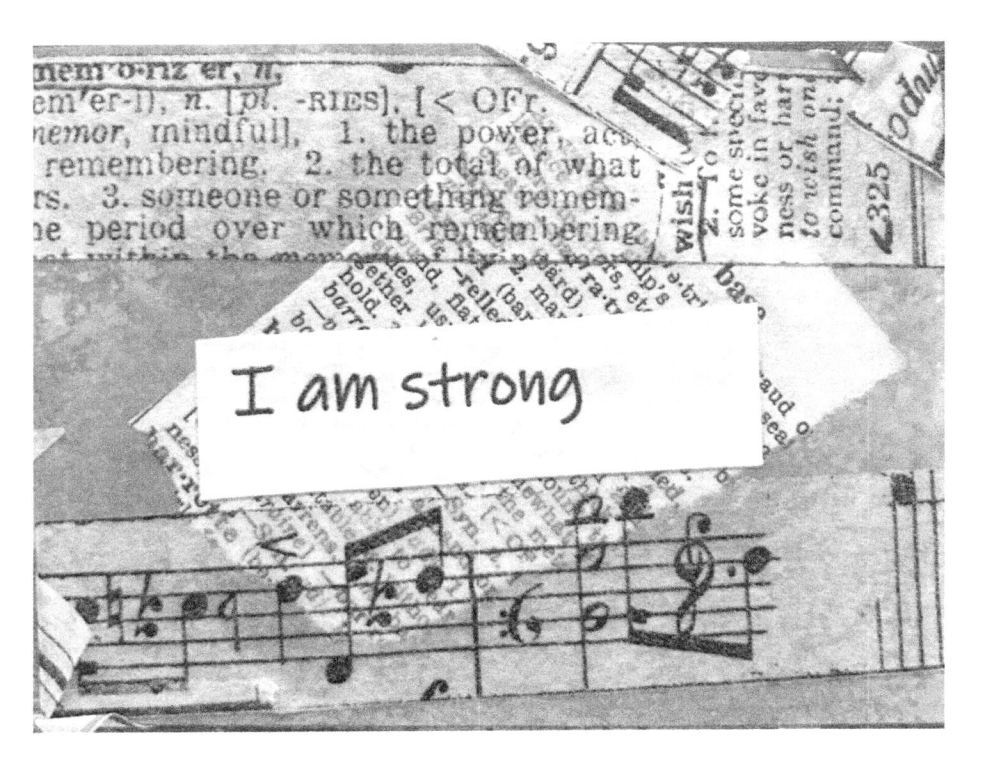

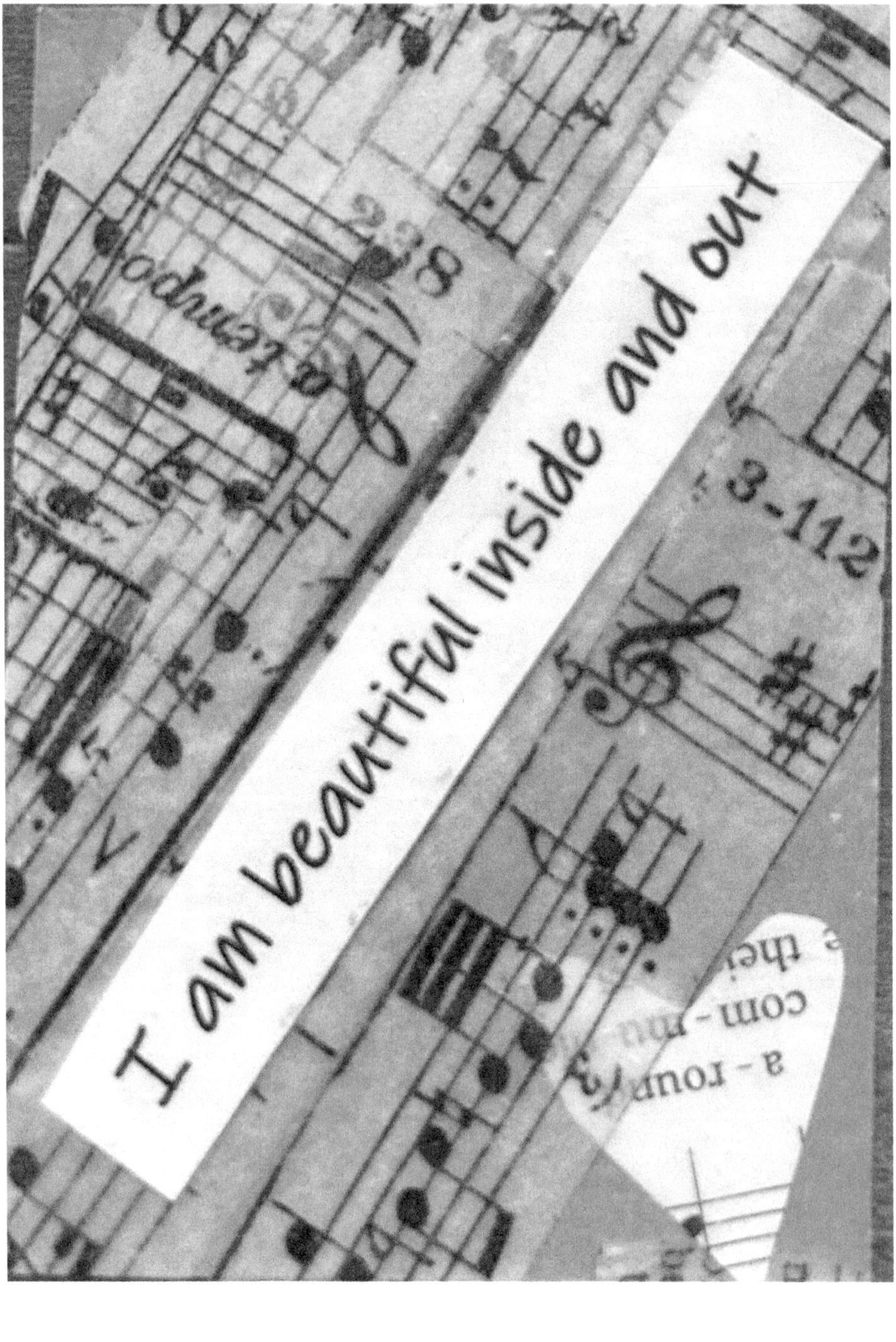
I am beautiful inside and out

Zoe

I deserve to be happy

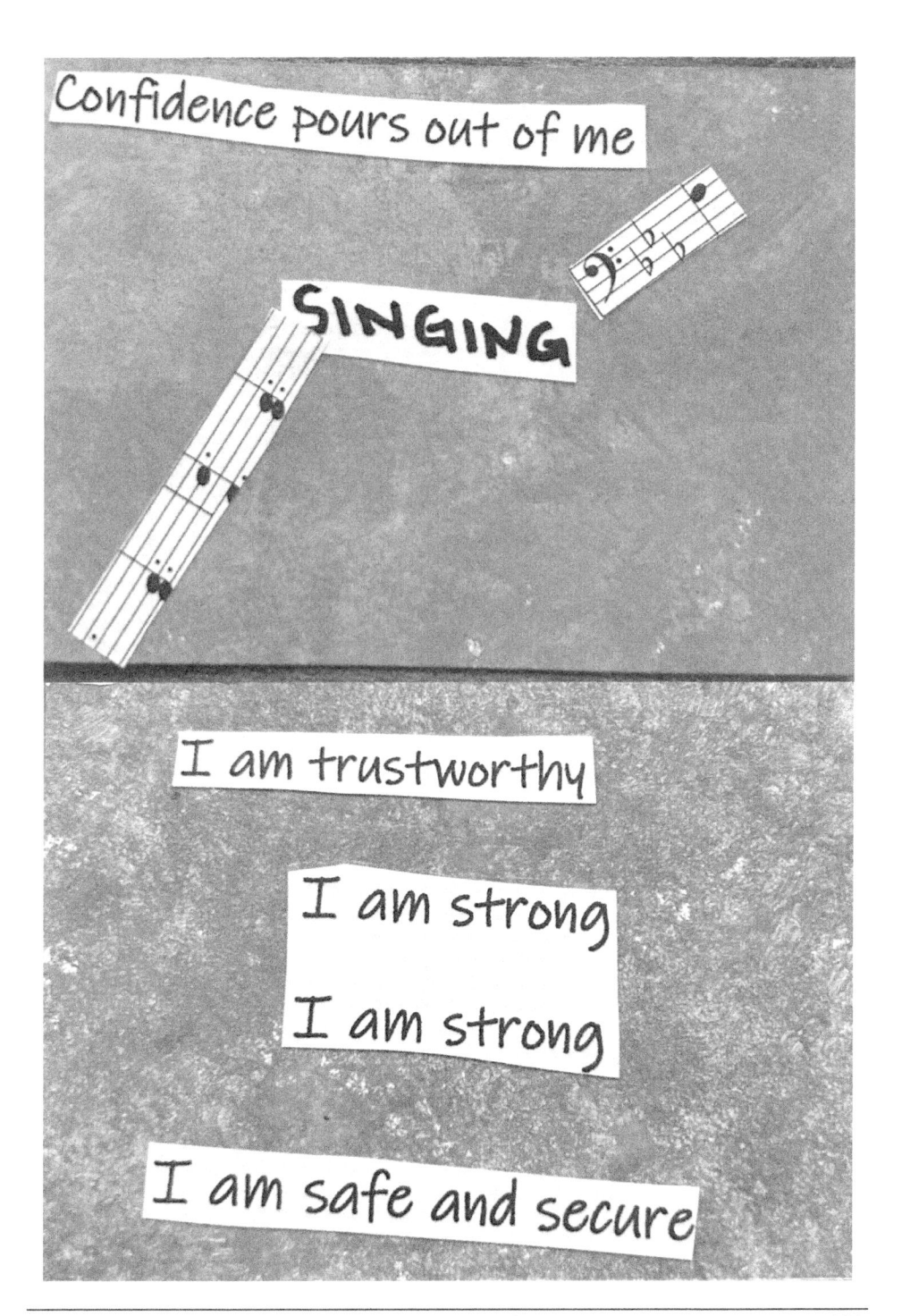

Confidence pours out of me

SINGING

I am trustworthy

I am strong

I am strong

I am safe and secure

Chapter 7

Empathy

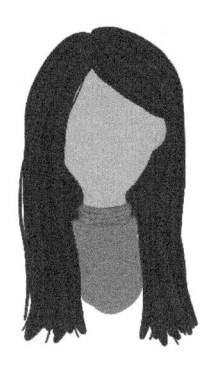

In this chapter, the young writers demonstrate empathy by responding to their peers' art and affirmations. Through their writings, they highlight and reflect on some of the affirmations presented in the previous chapter. These responses allow us to understand the writers' intentions and thoughts when creating their affirmation cards. Moreover, this chapter allows us to read the authors' reactions to their peers' art and affirmations. This exercise in personal and communal empathy reveals the impact that our words can have on others. These interactions create a space of connection and mutual understanding, where the young writers support and inspire each other.

Fartun

I am helpful.
I live in worries.
I give up easily.
I love myself

I am helpful; when you need my help, I will come and help you. Even though I am busy, I will come and help you. When I clean my house and cook, I leave behind what I am doing. I have a friend who helps with her sister and brother. I will stay with her until her mother comes back from work, and I will leave her house at 12:00, and I will go home and clean my house. When I am done, I will go to sleep because I have school in the morning.

In response to Fartun

The maps remind me of how I got lost on Thanksgiving Day. At night. My parents took me to Garner to get my hair done. Getting home was hard because I did not know how to translate the words from the GPS map. The lines confused me. I was stressed because my head hurt from getting my hair done. I could not translate well. They yelled at me: "How can you speak English and not know how to translate the directions in Swahili?" I am not good at translating maps and directions words. "X miles until X." I don't know, just tell me where to go.

-Kevine

"I give up easily" - I feel that

-Kevine

Iqra

Practice makes progress

Practice makes progress because when you practice, you will learn what you practice. In my Agricultural Science class, we got the FFA creed. The first was to memorize the FFA creed. Second was to read from the paper. Third was to fill in the blanks. I chose the first one because I want to give it a try. My teacher gave us 3 weeks. First, I didn't focus for the first 2 weeks. When I looked at the paragraphs, it was very long. Then I started.

In response to Iqra

This affirmation reminds me of a dream and reminds me of the color. I feel good when I look at this affirmation card.

-Fartun

This affirmation reminds me of a violin. Maps remind me of teammates. I feel good. I like the color. My favorite parts are the violin and the paper.

-Kevine

Kevine

I am a positive person

I am always in the mood.
People enjoy being around me.
Some people don't.
I make people's day.
My friends are comfortable around me.
I make my friends feel safe.

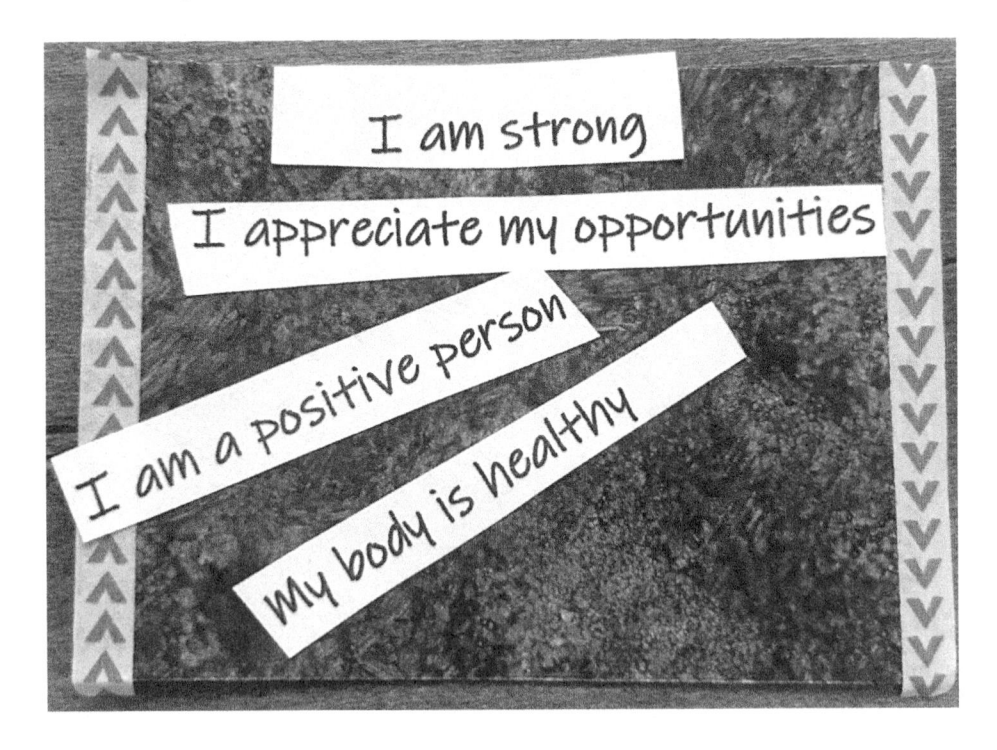

I am strong
I appreciate my opportunities
I am a positive person
My body is healthy

In response to Kevine

Kevine's card said, "I am strong" and I related to it. I feel like I should say this to myself because I don't say these words a lot. I could use it at school because my classes are hard. I can give up easily sometimes with friendships and school so this could help me.

-Fartun

I connected with this because I am a positive person. A positive person can help other people and they are confident in what they are doing. I am a positive person too; I help other people when they want. When I don't feel like doing something, I say some positive words to myself. Having homework every single day is hard, so then I must remember Kevine's card says that says "I am a positive person."

-Iqra

Rebecca

I believe in myself

Come to new school,
and to learn.
Met new people
and make new friends.
Speak a new language all of this
because I believe in myself.

In response to Rebecca

While reading Rebecca's affirmation, I was very connected to it. When I came to America, I did not speak English at all, just like her. She did not speak English. This was hard because people at school were a little bit judgmental. They judge you maybe because you don't speak the same language as them or because you come from another country rather than America. It's depressing, I remember a time in my math class in middle school. There was a girl who was popular in that class. She would come up to my friend's face and tell her, "You are very ugly." My friend did not understand what she was saying because she did not speak or understand English, just like me. I understand what Rebecca is saying. Believing in yourself is important if you know you can do it! I believed that I could speak English, and now I do. It's not perfectly fine, but I can speak English, and this all happened because I believed in myself.

   -Zoe

Her art reminds me of my own card. I had the same affirmation as her. I feel empathy when I look at this affirmation card. My favorite part about it is she believed in herself in a new country.

   -Zehra

Solange

I appreciate my opportunities ♥

Coming to America has given me a lot of opportunities that I would not have had or even gotten in Tanzania. I'm so happy to have all these changes that I know other people wish they had and I'm so grateful to be able to experience all of them. Such as being able to graduate high school and getting scholarships and having a future instead of getting married at such an early age.

In response to Solange

The affirmation of Solange was an appreciation of opportunities. I liked how thankful she was and appreciated her opportunities in the USA. This reminded me to stop and appreciate the opportunities I got as an immigrant to the USA. She reminded me that I appreciate what I got and know the worth of what I got in life. I won't have any regrets later in life when I lose them. I think it's normal in this life to forget to look to outside our window and miss beauty out there. I hope I remember this affirmation later in life because I want to be thankful for everything that I have.

   -Zehra

I feel so happy that she is aware of opportunities and thankful for it. My favorite part is when she says she is appreciative of the future in the USA instead of getting married at such an early age.

   -Zehra

Her piece reminds me of the opportunities that I have. It reminds me of my worth. I feel connected. Coming to America has given me a lot of opportunities that I would not have gotten in Tanzania.

   -Zoe

Zehra

I am strong

When I decided to train with weights in school, I had zero confidence in myself. I never thought I could lift a single bar, but when I went into it deeply and started to JUST BELIEVE IN MYSELF, I was able to do it. I never felt this strong mentally and physically. I remember a specific event when I had to lift a heavy weight for an important school grade. At that moment, I didn't have anything else to do but to believe in myself. I believe that if people believe in themselves, they will be unstoppable. If people believe in themselves, nothing can stop them but their mental power. I believe that if I didn't believe in myself at that moment, I couldn't lift that weight. I think everything ends in your mind. In your thoughts. We as human beings, we are capable of everything. Yeah, so believe in yourself and you'll see the power of yourself. ♥

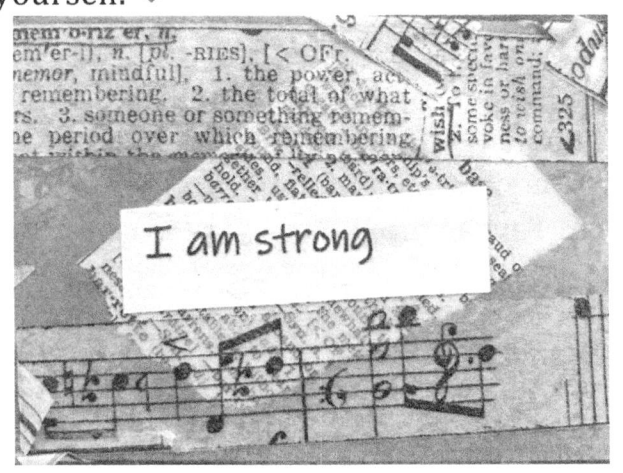

In response to Zehra

Zehra's piece reminds me of when I was in middle school and the struggles I went through. I feel connected to the phrase.

-Solange

Zoe

Singing

The reason why I chose "singing" is because I really love and enjoy singing. It makes me feel delighted and blessed.

I live in joy

The reason why I chose "living in joy" is because I love to laugh, I don't like negativity, and I hate being unhappy. I have been stressed. I know things happen, and things get hard, but I try to make my life bright. I just learned that if I want things to be positive, I must be first. That's why "I live in joy." God is also here with me too.

In response to Zoe

I feel good and happy
She sings because she loves to sing
And she feels happy and blessed to laugh
And to live with joy in God is a blessing and I think
Her favorite thing to do is to sing
I feel happy when I sing too because I enjoy it
I like to sing worship songs like: "Holy Night"
And "We Three Kings."

-Rebecca

Zoe's art reminded me of the younger me when I was in choir because I had a strict teacher, and she was mean and rude. She always made me feel like I couldn't sing but I loved singing. I really enjoyed going to the choir with my two best friends, Faines and Esther, and getting to stand in front of a lot of people and sing for God. It made me feel so proud of myself, but having someone as strict as my teacher always gave me a hard time. Sometimes she made me feel so unconfident to be able to sing, but I did not want to leave the choir because it was also something I was positive about and loved very much. I had to find my confidence and keep going with the work I was doing. My friends and mom helped me continue my passion and love for singing.

-Solange

Chapter 8

Vision Boards

Creating a vision board is a powerful tool for manifesting dreams and goals that provides inspiration, focus and clarity.

Eupiphanie

Iqra

PINEHURST 1895

You can't turn back the clock, but you can pause it for a day or two.

For more than a century, the mild climate, gracious service and unhurried pace have drawn folks to Pinehurst Resort. Whether you prefer to take a leisurely bike ride through our New England-style Village, to indulge yourself at our luxurious spa, or to rock away the afternoon under the ceiling fans on our veranda, you and your family will find much more than a historic retreat. You'll find time for each other.

Golf or Spa Escape $159*
One Round of Golf or
One Spa Treatment
Accommodations
Breakfast

Kevine

Ornella

FOR SUCCESSFUL LIVING
Life's simple pleasures...
Perfection
Bedroom
Study
Dn
Loft
Stair tower, open to below
cond floor
Covered porch
Great room
Master bedroom
Special Moments
Kitchen
Laundry
Up
Mudroom
Entry
Guest bedroom
Master bath
UB THE BOTTLE
D DISCOVER SCENT

Rebecca

Duke Gardens was named among the nation's "insanely beautiful public gardens" by The Huffington Post.

STRATEGIC PLAN GOAL:
BE RECOGNIZED AS ONE OF THE BEST PUBLIC GARDENS IN AMERICA

'Aveyron' F210139
Z3-7S&W MAY HT20- SP5

Salwa

Sarah

Solange

Sophia

Wile

Chapter 9

Justice

In this chapter, the writers share poems about justice. During the writing sessions, we reflected on how culture interacts with our perception of justice, how our experiences influence this vision, and how we interpret the world. Their writings show us how their experiences have shaped their understanding of the world and their concept of justice. Their voices remind us that justice is not a universal concept but interwoven with our identities, cultures, and experiences. They challenge us to question existing structures and systems and imagine a more just and inclusive world.

Being a Black Person in USA
Eupiphanie

Black people have the hardest life in the United States
because of their skin color,
their intelligence
and their hard work.
US policies need to change
because they can't arrest
Black people
just because
they suspect something.

Congo
Eupiphanie

We all know
that Congo is a big country
that has a lot of treasures.
Every country
wants Congo's treasure
which isn't fair
because every country
has their own treasures
and Congo isn't trying
to take them away from them.
Please.
We need justice
for Congo
and its treasure.

School
Eupiphanie

School needs to understand
that every student
and teacher
have hardships outside school
and they need to try
to understand people
because not every day
you wake up
feeling happy.

People Want Justice
Iqra

Freedom of religion in every country.
People want justice

Don't judge people by their looks.
People want justice

Don't treat people for how they speak.
People want justice

Don't take advantage of people
who can't speak your language.
People want justice

One country is always a powerful country.
People want justice

We Are All Equal
Kevine

Some students are smart and understand
Other students are not because they don't understand
We are all equal.

Some people wear expensive clothes
Others wear cheap clothes
We are all equal.

Some people speak different languages
Some people speak more than one language
We are all equal.

Some people live in a city full of a lot of stuff
Others live in a city but they don't have
what other people or other countries have
We are all equal.

I think for me
all people are equal
because even though everybody doesn't have the same things
we all live in the same world
We should love each other.

Injustice Has To Go
Ornella

Justice
should be served
everywhere.
When
are we gonna get
justice?

Justice Should Be Served
Ornella

Equal rights,
fair and true
we need justice.

> *The arc of the moral universe*
> *is long,*
> *But it ends*
> *towards justice.*

-Dr. Martin Luther King Jr.

We Are All Equal
Rebecca

Some students are going to school
because they want to learn more
Other students
can't go to school
We are all equal

Some people wear short clothes
Others wear long clothes
We are all equal

Some people live in the USA
Others live in Congo
We are all equal

We all live in the same world
so we should all love each other.

See Life Clearly Without Our Judgement and Filters
Salwa

This is what I want in the world for justice:

Stop judging.

Everybody's equal and no one is hungry.

Love each other.

Stop talking bad things about other people.

Respect each other.

Stop saying that Africans are poor just because they are from a different country.

Stop treating Black people like they are bad.

The USA needs to stop stealing from Congo!

Stop body-shaming people.

Let's have peace and love for everybody.

Color means nothing!

We Are All Equal
Sarah

Some students understand English
Other students don't understand English
We are all equal.

Some people wear dresses
Others wear hoodies and pants
We are all equal.

Some people speak Arabic
Some people speak English
We are all equal.

Some people live in an apartment
Others live in a house
We are all equal.

                    We are all equal
        So we shouldn't be mean to each other.

My Race Does Not Define Who I Am
Solange

We live in a world that has many different races
from 100 and more different countries.

I personally think people with darker skin
get injustice the most,
especially here
in America.

A Black kid can be walking in a store
and a white person can call them out for stealing
or even go up to them and tell them to get out
because they think they are gonna steal.
Not everyone that's Black is a thief.

I would like for Black people to get justice
because you can't just assume
that someone is a thief
just because of their skin color,
and that happens to many Black people.

They end up going to jail
for things they never did
and they get sentenced to jail
for like 40 or 20 years and years.
Later, they find out

they never committed the crime.

They ruin their lives being in jail for half their lives
and never even giving them justice at all.
There are some people who even die in jail
For things they really never even did.

Stop the Violence
Sophia

Some students are scared of going to school
because they are scared of getting bullied.
Other students are the bullies.
We should all get along
and stop the bullying.

Some people wear hijabs.
Others wear clothes that show their body.
We are all equal.

Some people have an accent.
Some don't.
We are all equal.

Some people live in Africa, Afghanistan, and Jordan.
Others live in America.
We are all equal.

There are bad things, like bullying and discrimination
people should stop.
We want people to show love to one another.

We Are All Equal
Wile

Some students are born in America
                Other students are from different countries
        We are all equal.

Some people wear modest clothing because of their religion
                    Others wear what they want
        We are all equal.

Some people speak different languages
                  Some people speak one language
        We are all equal.

Some people have lived in different countries
                Others have only lived in one country
        We are all equal.

We all equal so we shouldn't judge people
before we get to know them.

Chapter 10

Activism

In this chapter, the writers take a stance and compose letters of advocacy, urging readers to become aware of issues that hold deep significance to them. With passion and conviction, they express their heartfelt desires for change and heightened consciousness regarding topics such as religion, family, education, self-esteem, and interpersonal relationships. Through their words, they invite us to open our minds, challenge our preconceptions, and join them in their pursuit of understanding and transformation. As we delve into their letters, we are reminded of the strength that lies within each individual voice and the collective power we possess to effect meaningful change in our world.

Dear Faith People
Eve

Dear Faith People,

My name is Eve, and I am writing to you: faith people. Sometimes, people have trouble opening up about their faith to loved ones. Children grow up learning things about their families' faith and as they get older, they start to question their families' beliefs. They don't get the answers they are looking for. The answers aren't enough for them to not question more. Example from Eve: Eve grew up as a Muslim, and she started to question her faith. She didn't understand why some things in the Quran were allowed.

Even though it may be hard to not have your child believe what you believe, you should understand and support your kid. Sometimes people even kick their kids out. People who are supposed to follow their parents' faith should not be afraid to open up and see their parents' reaction because God is leading them, and He will bring people to help them in the future.

Respectfully,
Eve

Dear Sanderson
Kevine

Dear Sanderson,

My name is Afsa Kevine, and I am writing to you about the punishment of being tardy. This is important to me because sometimes I have a lot of places to be and the bus comes late. Also, some of us have parents who don't speak English, and they can't write notes for us to take to school. Being punished for being tardy should be important to others because we have problems and stuff to take care of outside of school. Something we can do to help those facing this issue is to change the time and the schedule of the school day. Another thing could be for the school to pay enough money to the bus drivers. Solving this issue would help the school community by making the school community feel better and not afraid of being punished for being tardy.

Sincerely,

Kevine

Dear Students
Rebecca

Dear Students,

My name is Rebecca, and I am writing to you about an issue that Sanderson's students need to change. Students need to stop talking about other people and be kind. They should stop acting rude and not look people up and down. I don't like it because it makes me, and others feel bad, and I just don't like it. Students should be kind to one another to build a better school community. Teachers and administrators should help foster good communication among students.

Thank you for your time,

Rebecca

Dear Sanderson
Solange

Dear Sanderson,

My name is Solange, and I am writing to you about the 20-minute bathroom rule. This is important to me because students have been complaining. Because some teachers take their anger at the students. Like in one of my classes, the teacher is so mean and even if it's an emergency, you can't use the bathroom at all. I think she should be kind as a teacher and let us use the bathroom if it's an emergency. Choice should be important to others because students should be able to use the bathroom when it is an emergency.

And then we have the tardy rule. What kind of madness has the world come to? There is no way these schools are here sending students to court because of being late! Most of the time it is the bus that's late, not even the students. And they still are marking us tardy, and that honestly needs to stop. Stressing students out about being sent to court! We already have things we are dealing with at home and now we gotta worry about being sent to court? That just sounds crazy to me! We students should be treated better than this.

Something we can do to help those facing this issue is to gather all the students in the big gym and talk about it with everyone together. Solving this issue would help the world by giving students the right to be able to talk about their choices and write about some school rules.

Sincerely,
Solange

Dear You
Wile

Dear You,

My name is Wile, and I am writing to you about individuality. This is important to me because it is good to care about yourself. This should be important to others because they should know that they matter. Something we can do to help those facing this issue is to let them know they matter, and they shouldn't listen to what others say about them. Solving this issue would help the world by remembering that sometimes other people's words can hurt you. You just need to ignore what people say about you.

Thank you for your time,
Wile

APPENDIX

Biographies
of Authors and Artists

Annointing

I'm Annointing and I'm from South Africa. I have 5 siblings! All of us can speak at least 2 languages. I'm a Christian and my faith is really important to me.

To tell you the truth, I'm not the biggest fan of writing. But if writing can make people happy, then I'm all for it! I wrote about my experiences coming to the project's sessions. Art is a whole different story. I love the messiness and even the pain that can come with creating art. There's nothing better than just letting loose and making some crazy, wild art. I like to draw or paint whatever comes to mind, without any rules or limits. I think writing and art are important because they give people a way to express their feelings. For me, writing and art are a way to share my own journey and story with others. I want people to see how far I've come and what I've been through.

Eupiphanie

Hi there! My name is Eupiphanie and I'm a 17-year-old from the beautiful country of Burundi ✉. One of my favorite things in the world is asking questions - I'm just so curious about everything!

When it comes to writing, I love how it lets me explore and share my life experiences. I enjoy writing about my own life and the things that happen to me. It's a great way for me to express myself. Art is another passion of mine, especially working with colors. I like creating art that's interesting, fun, and grabs people's attention. Mixing colors and coming up with cool designs brings me a lot of joy.

I think writing and art are both really important because they give me a sense of peace and calm. Life can be stressful sometimes, but when I'm being creative, I feel so much better. Writing and making art also helps me share my story with others. I think my life is kinda interesting, so I enjoy letting people know more about me and my experiences.

Fartun

My name is Fartun, and I am from Somali. My favorite thing about writing is that I can tell people my story to get it out of my head. I like to write about everything that I can share with people. Here are some other things about me: I grew up in Kenya but am from Somalia because my parents are from Somalia.

Iqra

My name is Iqra Saleh, and I am from Afghanistan. My favorite thing about writing is writing about something interesting. I like to write about everything and interesting things. My favorite thing about art is that we use color, and she teaches us new things. I like to create art because I learn new things. I think writing and art are important because it helps me think more. Writing and art help me share my story by using words and color. Here are some other things about me: I like playing badminton and I am 14 years old.

Kevine

My name is Afsa Kevine. My favorite thing about writing is being open. I like to write about what I feel and how I feel.

Ornella

Hi, my name is Ornella and I'm 15 years old. One of my favorite things to do is sleep! But when I'm not sleeping, I really love to write. Writing is so fun for me because I get to create my own worlds and characters. I can explore different ideas and feelings in my stories. It's a fun challenge to find just the right words to describe what I'm thinking. I feel myself improving at writing the more I do it.

When I write, it's like going into my own little world where no one disturbs me. I get so into it! Writing makes me smile, and it makes my friends and family smile too when they read my stories. You never know when being a good writer will come in handy in life.

Rebecca

My name is Rebecca, and I am from Tanzania. My favorite thing about writing is it can teach people about my story. I like to write about myself and stuff like that. I like to create art that relates to the sky. I think writing and art are important because they can make us express our feelings. Here are some things about me: I like to cook, clean the house, take care of my siblings, and live with my family.

Salwa

My name is Salwa-Nabintu. I am from Burundi, and I am sixteen years old. I am an amazing person, because I love seeing other people happy. I am a refugee from Burundi. I came here because my country had a war. I wanted to write for this book because I want people to know that being a refugee doesn't mean you are poor. I want people to know that Africa is beautiful.

Sarah

Hi, my name is Sarah and I'm from the country of Jordan. I'm 15 years old. In my free time, I love listening to my favorite music. I also really enjoy drawing. When I create art, I like it to have a deeper meaning. I want my drawings to make people think or feel something. Even though I'm young, I believe art can send a message and make a difference.

Solange

My name is Solange, and I am from Tanzania. My favorite thing about writing is that I get to express the way I feel. My favorite thing about art is that you can paint whatever you want. I like to create art that stands out. I think writing and art are important because I express myself. Writing and art help me share my story by sharing my feelings with others. Here are some things about me: I'm in a family of 10. I'm the second one.

Sophia

Hi, I'm Sophia and I'm from the country of Burundi. I'm 15 years old. I have a big family with 6 sisters and one brother. Two of my sisters are married now and my brother moved out with his wife.

One of my favorite things to do is drink boba tea. I enjoy it so much! But I also really love writing and drawing. Writing helps me express myself and share all the thoughts and feelings I have inside. Drawing is another way I can let my feelings out and show my creative side. I think writing and drawing are both so interesting because they connect people. They give us a voice to share ideas with each other. And the more I talk about my writing and art, the better I feel! It's such a positive outlet for me.

Wile

My name is Wile. My favorite thing about writing is writing. I like to write about myself. My favorite thing about art is everything. I like to create art that relates to the sky. I think writing and art are important because they can express our feelings.

Zehra

Hi, I'm Zehra. I'm 17 years old. I live with my mom and brother. We have a small family. I really like writing. It helps me share my feelings. When I write, I feel creative. It helps me understand myself better. Writing is a way for me to deal with stress. I have a lot I want to say.

I'm not super interested in art, but I do love music. I enjoy singing and playing the piano. Singing my favorite songs makes me really happy. I hope my music can make other people happy too and inspire them. Music lets me share my life journey with everyone.

Another thing I like is archery. I'm not totally sure what I want to do when I'm older. But I know I want to go back to Turkey someday, because that's where I'm from. For now, I'm just focused on doing the things I love and being true to myself.

Zoe

Hi, my name is Zoe and I'm from the beautiful country of Tanzania. I recently turned 18 years old. One of my favorite things to do is sing. I like to try new things and have new experiences.

When it comes to writing, I really enjoy the freedom of it. With writing, I can talk about whatever I want, especially things happening in my life. It's a peaceful activity for me. Writing lets me express what's in my heart. When I write about my life and my feelings, it helps me share my story with others.

Project Photos

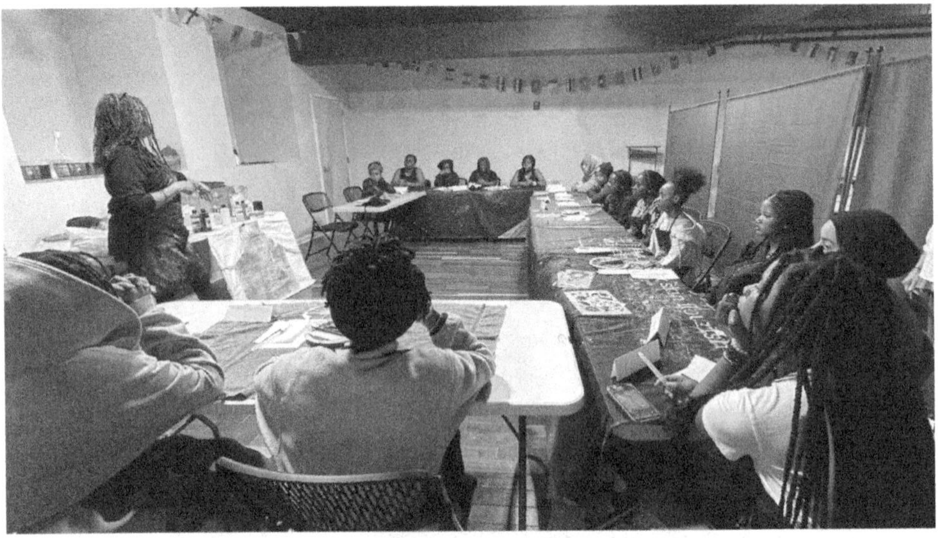

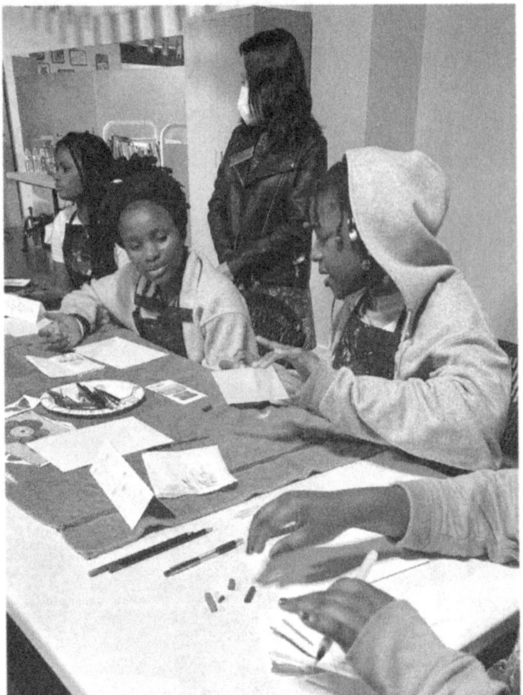

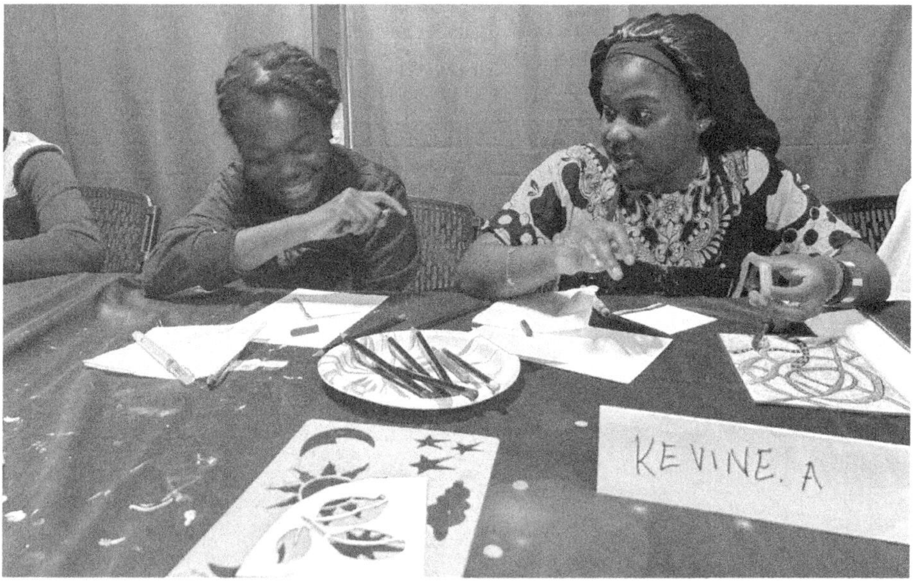
KEVINE. A

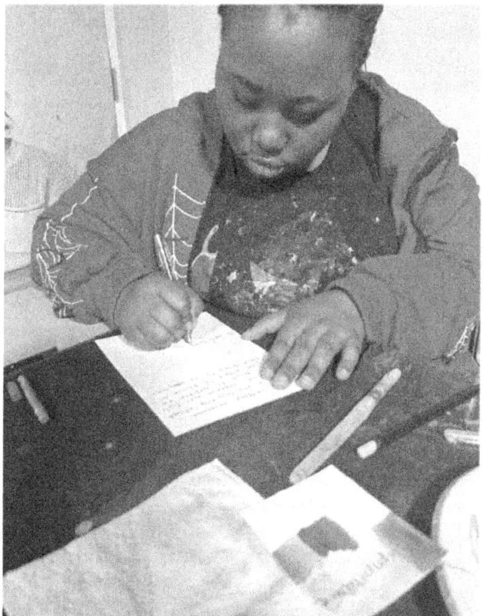

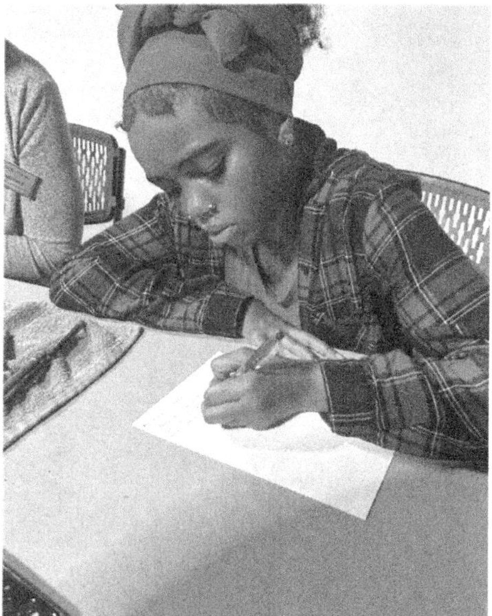

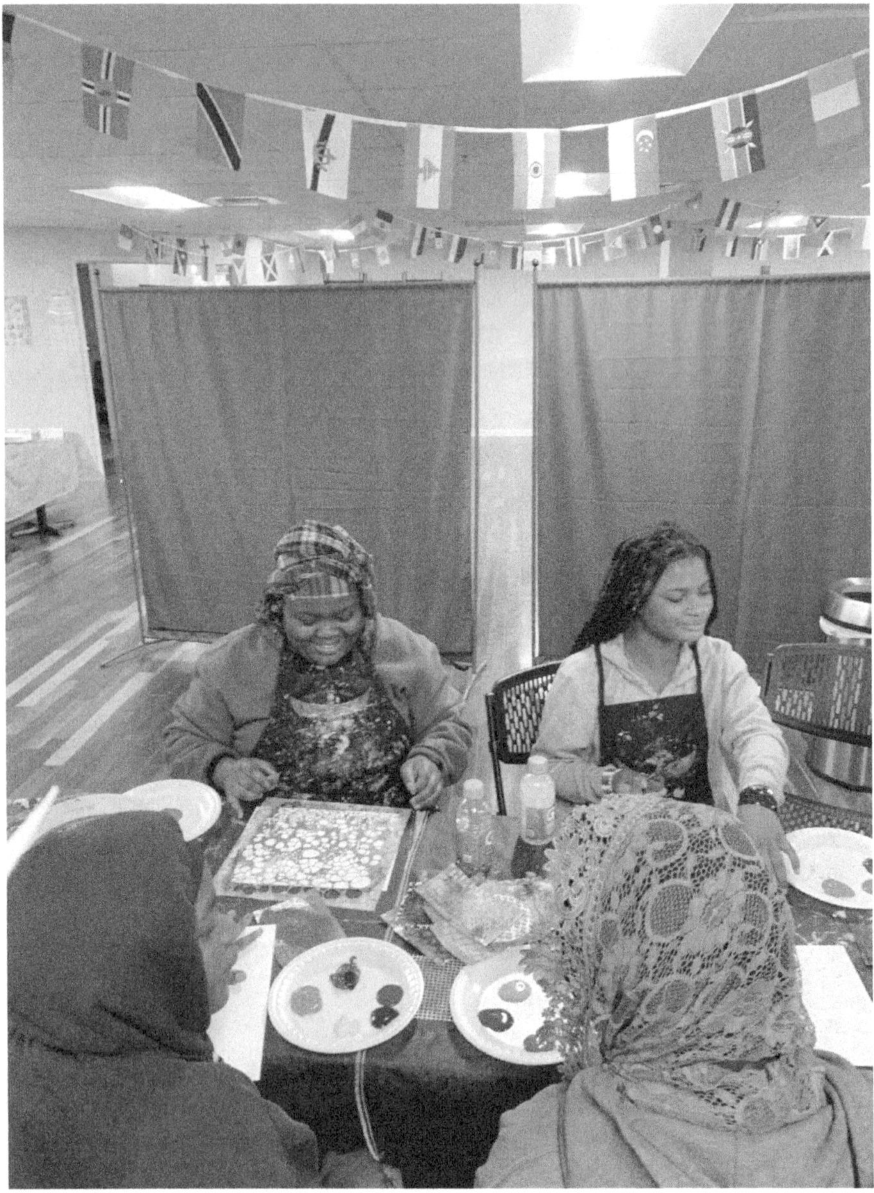

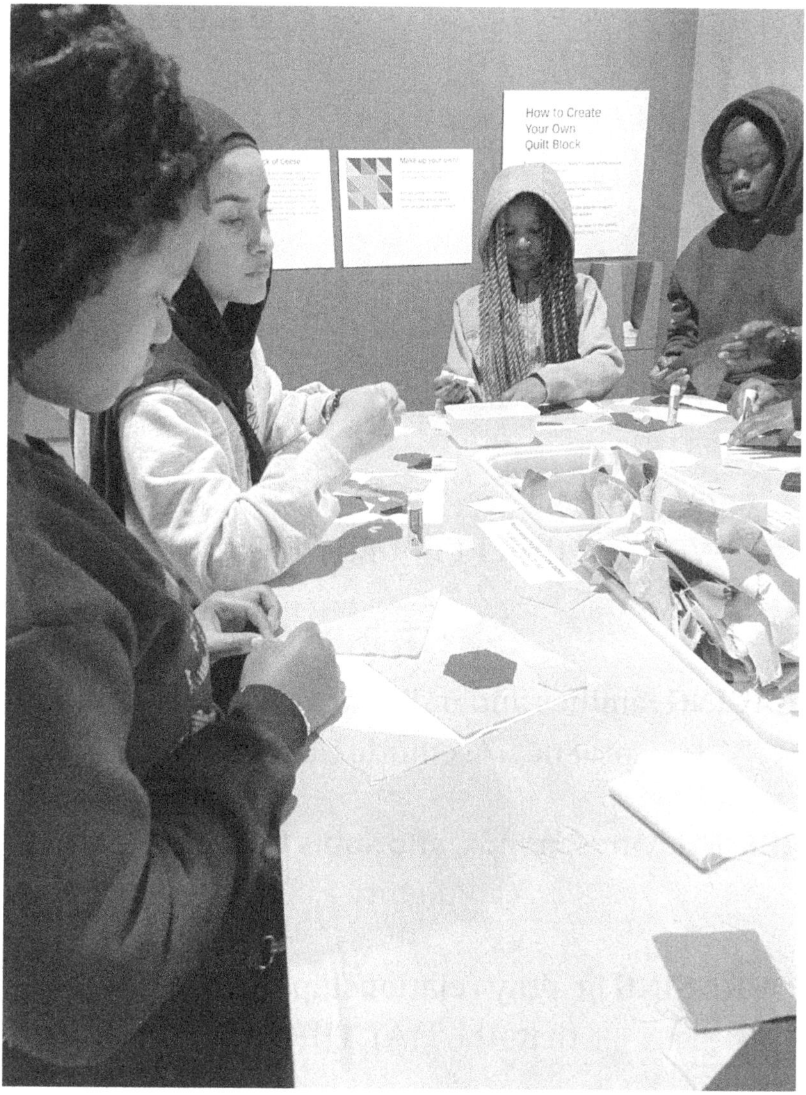
How to Create
Your Own
Quilt Block

About Refugee Hope Partners

WE LOVE OUR REFUGEE NEIGHBORS BY

ENGAGING families and individuals as they face cultural, practical & emotional hurdles

EQUIPPING hands, minds, and souls for independence with dignity

ENCOURAGING healthy relationships & spiritual growth so that ALL MAY THRIVE!

About the Founder and Executive Director:

About the Founder and Executive Director
Michele Suffridge

Michele is the founder and executive director of Refugee Hope Partners and has been serving refugees in the Triangle area of North Carolina since 2007. Michele has been married to her husband, Rick, for 37 years and is mom to five children. Through the years, Michele has sought ways to simply include the refugee community in her community. Her life has been greatly impacted by the amazing families she has come to know as friends and neighbors.

About the Director of High School & College Academics:
Anna Christian Allen

Anna Christian Allen is the Director of High School & College Academics for Refugee Hope Partners. As part of this role, she oversees the partnership between LCI and RHP. Prior to joining RHP, AC taught ESL as a National Board Certified Teacher and coached girls basketball in the Wake County Public School System for almost a decade. She has thoroughly enjoyed partnering with the LCI staff and watching the refugee participants write and display their creativity throughout this school year. In her free time, AC enjoys reading, following college basketball, and spending time with her family.

About the High School and College Academics Assistant:
Mary Greene

Mary Greene is the High School and College Academics Assistant for Refugee Hope Partners. As part of this role, she supports the partnership between LCI and RHP through participation in the monthly meetings. Prior to joining RHP Mary had various educational roles including High School teacher and coach and volunteer ESL teacher for refugee women. She has delighted in her time with the LCI collaboration as she watched the refugee participants flourish through discussion, writing and art. The end result is a gift for now and later, for participants and recipients. In her free time, Mary enjoys time with family and friends, being outdoors, a good nap and a good laugh.

About the North Carolina Museum of Art

North Carolina Museum of Art

At the North Carolina Museum of Art, we believe in the transformative power of art. Through the People's Collection, the state art collection that belongs to the citizens of North Carolina, and our 164-acre Park, we strive to create a sense of welcome and belonging.

Our collection galleries span more than 5,000 years, from antiquity to the present, and provides countless cultural experiences for the people of our state and beyond. The Museum Park showcases the connection between art and nature through site-specific works of art and notable programming. Both are free to visit.

We also offer changing special exhibitions, classes, lectures, family activities, films, dance performances, and concerts.

About the NCMA Director of Outreach
and Audience Engagement:
Angela Lombardi

Angela Lombardi is the Director of Outreach and Audience Engagement at the North Carolina Museum of Art where she leads a dynamic team of programmers who create public events for all ages. With a focus on amplifying the talents of local artists, she engages young people in rural communities across NC through NCMA's signature outreach project, the Artist Innovation Mentorship Program. Lombardi is the Vice Chair of the City of Raleigh Public Art and Design Board and maintains an active artistic practice. She comes to her museum career by way of studio art, graduating from Hunter College in New York. She continued her training in academic drawing and sculpture at the Florence Academy of Art. Upon moving to North Carolina in 2006, she worked as a teaching artist and started a mobile studio camp for middle school students as well as creating educational programming directly with artists for four years as manager of education and outreach at Artspace in downtown Raleigh.

About the Artist Innovation Mentorship (AIM) Program Manager
Ashlee Moody, MFA

Ashlee Moody is the Program Manager for the NC Museum of Art's outreach initiative, "Artist Innovation Mentorship Program". Ashlee earned her MFA from NC State University where she spent her academic career advocating that principles of creative placemaking offer new ways of thinking about sustainability and community engagement as part of the development of long-lasting art education programs. Prior to joining the NCMA team, the local Durham native has served in the art community for several years as a teacher, mentor, consultant, and AmeriCorps Vista. With her strong background in K-12 education, art education, and art research, she hopes to one-day build and passionately lead empowering learning spaces that encourage people's ability to innovate and create within community environments.

About the Resident Artist of this project:
Maria Geary

Maria Geary is a Durham, NC based mixed media and fiber artist with a passion for visual journaling. She creates bold and expressive art and is influenced by her journaling practice and social issues. She incorporates texture and found objects in her work and encourages viewers to contemplate the feelings the art unveils.

About the Literacy and Community Initiative

LITERACY AND COMMUNITY INITIATIVE

The Literacy and Community Initiative (LCI), a collaboration between NC State's College of Education and the Friday Institute for Educational Innovation, partners with community-based organizations to examine and empower youth voices.

Mission: Our mission is to amplify student voices through student publications, advocacy, and leadership.

Our motto is **Write, Engage, and Lead.**
Write: Students' writing process and publication on their narratives and educational experiences improve literacy learning and amplify student voices.
Engage: Students' engagement with literacy in community-based organizations empower multiple educational stakeholders to learn with and from underserved youth to achieve educational equity.
Lead: Reading, sharing, and publishing narratives enable youth to lead and inspire communities to act and advocate for underserved youth.

At the Literacy and Community Initiative, we believe that literacy is:

Shared. We believe that the literacy work with and among our community partnerships allows multiple stakeholders in education (professors, teachers, students, community leaders, family members, etc.) to make visible the assets of marginalized students within and beyond the community.

An advancement for educational equity. We believe literacy is powerful and liberatory: reading, writing, and speaking are not just tools, but values that lead to personal and social change especially for marginalized populations.

A vehicle for community engagement. We believe that literacy is a vehicle for critical thinking and action for the self, community, and world. Therefore, literacy leads to increased self-esteem, critical action, and global citizenship.

Leadership. We believe that literacy is a form of leadership, and when literacy lies in the hands of our most vulnerable populations, we can close the achievement and opportunity gaps starting with our students who lead the way.

Visit www.go.ncsu.edu/lci for more information.

About the Founder and Director:

Dr. Crystal Chen Lee

Dr. Crystal Chen Lee is an Associate Professor of English Education in the College of Education at North Carolina State University. Her research lies at the nexus of literacy, marginalized youth, and community organizations. She is the founding director of the Literacy & Community Initiative at NC State University. Her work has been featured nationally and internationally, and she has published in books and journal articles such as *Urban Education, Teachers College Record, Reading Research Quarterly, Journal of Literacy Research, Journal of Adolescent and Adult Literacy, English Journal, Teaching and Teacher Education*, and *International Journal of Qualitative Studies in Education*. Her current work has been supported by grants from the National Council of Teachers of English, Engaged Scholarship Consortium, and National Science Foundation.

Dr. Lee is very excited about this project with Refugee Hope Partners and is consistently encouraged by the youth writers. One of her greatest passions is empowering students' voices through reading, writing, and speaking. A child of immigrant parents from Taiwan, Dr. Lee began her teaching experience as a high school English teacher in New Jersey. She received her Ed.D. in Curriculum and Teaching from Columbia University, in New York City.

About the Co-Director:
Dr. José Picart

Dr. Jose Picart is the Deputy Director of the Friday Institute for Educational Innovation at North Carolina State University, the co-director of the Literacy and Community Initiative, and a Professor of Counselor Education in the College of Education.

Dr. Jose Picart completed his undergraduate degree at West Point, the United States Military Academy. Following his graduation from West Point, Dr. Picart served as a commissioned military officer for 28 years, rising through various command and staff positions to the rank of Colonel. He earned his Master of Science and Doctoral degrees in experimental cognitive psychology from the University of Oklahoma in Norman. He served for over 16 years on the faculty in the Department of Behavioral Sciences and Leadership at West Point, culminating with his appointment as the Director of Psychology Studies. In 1994, Dr. Picart was the recipient of a prestigious American Council on Education (ACE) Fellowship.

At NC State University, Dr. Picart has served as the Vice Provost for Academic Programs and Services, Vice Provost for Diversity and Inclusion, as well as Interim Dean of the College of Education. In 2015, Dr. Picart was recognized as a Professor Emeritus and Distinguished Faculty Alumnus in a ceremony at West Point. His current research and writings are focused on intrinsic motivation, self-determination theory, and leadership for campus diversity.

About the Research Collaborator
Dr. Angela Wiseman

Angela Wiseman is an Associate Professor of Literacy Education and a Provost Faculty Fellow for Global Leadership at NC State University. In addition, she has an appointment as a scholar of multiliteracies research at the University of Tampere, Finland and is affiliated faculty of the Center for Visual Literacies at San Diego State University. Her research focus is connected to responding, understanding, and analyzing children's literature through interdisciplinary projects that incorporate trauma-informed approaches, visual research methods, classroom learning, and community engagement that are grounded in social justice. A key aspect of her scholarship involves using qualitative visual and multimodal research methodologies for analyzing illustrations in children's picture books as well as visual responses and artifacts (i.e., sketches, digital images), usually in response to children's literature.

Angela serves on the Board of Directors for the Children's Literature Assembly which is a professional community of children's literature scholars within the organization of the National Council of Teachers of English. Angela is the co-PI of the grant Cultural Investigation and Digital Representation for Educators (CIDRE), which is a professional development program for in-service teachers that uses technology tools and literacy approaches in international contexts. CIDRE is funded by the Triangle Community Foundation's Borchardt Fund.

About the Visiting Scholar
Dr. Demet Seban

Dr. Demet Seban is a visiting scholar at NCSU from Turkey. She is an Associate Professor of Elementary Education in the Faculty of Education at Alanya Alaaddin Keykubat University. She was supported with a grant by the Turkish government and received her Ph.D. in Curriculum and Instruction from Indiana University in 2006.

Her research interests include teaching writing at elementary grades, critical literacy, identity, diversity, equity and social justice in teacher education.

Dr. Seban is very happy and honored to have an opportunity to observe this project and meet very precious people.

LCI Project Coordinator & Graduate Research Assistant:

María Heysha Carrillo Carrasquillo, M. Ed.

Heysha is a doctoral student in the Department of Teacher Education and Learning Sciences who specializes in Educational Equity at NC State. She is a Puerto Rican bilingual educator who has worked in North Carolina for a decade, teaching in schools and facilitating programs in community-based organizations. She received her M.Ed. in Early Childhood Intervention and Family Studies at the University of North Carolina at Chapel Hill and her B.A. in Elementary Education with a concentration in teaching English to Spanish speakers and a minor in Italian and French from the University of Puerto Rico at Río Piedras.

LCI Undergraduate Research Assistant:
Hannah Savariyar

Hannah Savariyar is a third-year undergraduate student at NC State University pursuing a degree in elementary education with a special education add-on. She is also a Teaching Fellow, a program that offers opportunities for students around North Carolina to become strong educators and leaders. Originally from Cary, NC, Hannah aspires to be an elementary school teacher who promotes inclusion within her classroom and allows all her students to share their unique life experiences with their peers and the world. Hannah currently works as an undergraduate research assistant for the Literacy and Community Initiative.

LCI Undergraduate Research Assistant:
Haven Hall

Haven Hall is in her final year at NC State University studying secondary English education. Following graduation, she hopes to stay in Wake County to teach high school English. At NC State, she is in the English Honors Program as well as being a University Ambassador. In addition to these programs, she volunteers at Neighbor to Neighbor, a community center in downtown Raleigh that is focused on educational equity. Her time there has made her a firm believer in the importance of community spaces, like Refugee Hope Partners. Haven currently works as an undergraduate research assistant for the Literacy and Community Initiative.

About the North Carolina State University College of Education

NC STATE UNIVERSITY

Mission: The College of Education is a voice of innovation in teaching and lifelong learning. We prepare professionals who educate and lead. Our inquiry and practice reflect integrity, a commitment to social justice and the value of diversity in a global community.

Vision: We lead the transformation of education. We ensure access and success for each and every learner in North Carolina and beyond. We produce innovative educational research. We solve the pressing challenges of education.

Visit https://ced.ncsu.edu/ for more information.

About the Department of Teacher Education and Learning Sciences

NC STATE UNIVERSITY

Mission:
The Department of Teacher Education and Learning Sciences advances education through scholarship, leadership, and advocacy. We prepare professionals who are committed to equity and social justice, have deep content knowledge, demonstrate strong working knowledge of effective pedagogies, and realize the potential of digital technologies to enhance learning.

We shape the field of education by engaging in research that addresses current challenges, and by participating in cross-disciplinary work that deals with real problems in forward-looking ways. The department exemplifies an innovative merging of teacher education and the learning sciences that results in new pathways for teaching, scholarship, leadership, and service. The preparation that our students receive is unmatched in scope, priorities, and outcomes, assuring that our graduates are able to make profound contributions to education and society.

About the Friday Institute of Educational Innovation

NC STATE UNIVERSITY Friday Institute for Educational Innovation

Mission: Advancing K-12 education through innovation in teaching, learning and leadership, we bring together students, teachers, researchers, policymakers and educational professionals to foster collaborations that improve education for all learners.

Vision: All learners are prepared to succeed in a rapidly changing world.

We *think and do* in order to:

- **EDUCATE** by conducting professional learning, research and evaluation.
- **INNOVATE** by designing supports, tools and structures for educational change.
- **INSPIRE** by convening and catalyzing stakeholders to inform standards, policy and practice.

Made in the USA
Middletown, DE
10 April 2024